Confident Cyber Security

Confident Cyber Security

*The essential insights and
how to protect from threats*

SECOND EDITION

Jessica Barker

KoganPage

First published in Great Britain and the United States in 2020 by Kogan Page Limited
Second edition 2023

2nd Floor, 45 Gee Street
London
EC1V 3RS
United Kingdom

122 W 27th St, 10th Floor
New York, NY 10001
USA

4737/23 Ansari Road
Daryaganj
New Delhi 110002
India

www.koganpage.com

ISBNs
Hardback   978 1 3986 1194 8
Paperback   978 1 3986 1192 4
Ebook   978 1 3986 1193 1

British Library Cataloguing-in-Publication Data

A CIP record for this book is available from the British Library.

Library of Congress Control Number

2020941948

Typeset by Integra Software Services, Pondicherry
Print production managed by Jellyfish
Printed and bound by CPI Group (UK) Ltd, Croydon CR0 4YY

To my parents, for always being there for me. To my husband, for weathering the storms and watching the sunrise with me.

And to everyone in the cyber security community – including those of you who are just joining us. Let's keep learning, sharing and making the world a safer place.

Contents

An introduction to cyber security

'You can't work in cyber security unless you are very technical.'
'Users are the weakest link in cyber security.'
'Hackers are all criminals!'
'Cybercrime is targeted. It's only the concern of
governments and big business.'
'No one would target me; my data is not worth anything!'

These myths, and many more, plague cyber security. In this book, we will see why all of the above statements are false. We will demystify cyber security, and show the breadth and depth of the field; how it encompasses not just computer science, but also psychology, sociology, physical security, behavioural economics, marketing, design, education and much, much more.

Cyber security is a topic that cuts across pretty much every area of life. Government, healthcare, politics, fashion, sports, the media, big business, small business, charities, education – you name it, it is affected by cyber security. It is a fascinating, challenging, fast-paced field that changes every day, but at the same time is concerned with issues that have been a part of human life for centuries. In the last few years, awareness has grown phenomenally. Cyber security issues make national news on a seemingly daily basis, and it has become a boardroom and household subject of conversation.

Having been working in this industry for over ten years, I've witnessed this rise in awareness alongside a growth in understanding of the diversity of the topic. I have always worked on the human side of cyber security; I am passionate about raising awareness of cyber security, positively influencing people's behaviours online so they operate in a more secure way, measuring and advancing organizational cyber security culture, and translating technical messages for a non-technical audience. When I started in the field, this was very much a niche area of the industry and I would frequently have to explain to my peers in the community what it meant to work on the human side, and why people are an important dimension of this field. That is no longer the case: working on the human side of cyber security has become pretty mainstream within the industry. There has been an explosion in understanding that people are a fundamental part of cyber security, whether from the perspective of analysing the motivations and profiles of cybercriminals to designing security products to be more user-friendly, from recognizing what makes us so susceptible to social engineering to how we can better communicate cyber security messages to be more mindful of pedagogy.

When I was a teenager in the early 1990s, first experiencing the internet, I would never have expected that I would go on to have a successful career in a technology field – let alone the field of cyber security itself. This was, understandably, not even remotely on the radar of my school's career guidance professional. I was interested in technology, a little, but I didn't think I was capable of a career there. I was more interested in people, and disciplines related to understanding themes of society: history, English literature and sociology.

Later, having finished my PhD and not knowing what to do, I was headhunted by a cyber security consultancy. I had no idea what cyber security was or how someone who saw themselves as non-technical could be relevant to the field, but I was keen to find out. The UK Government had not long since released their strategy on cyber security and it was obvious that it was becoming more of a priority for them. The role was to involve carrying out cyber security assessments of organizations, and interviewing people about how they work with technology and understand risk – so the skills I had developed during my academic career were relevant. I was ready for a change, and excited to learn something new, so I took the job.

Entering the field of cyber security is a steep learning curve. However, what I immediately loved about the subject was how much there is to learn and how new challenges can emerge every day. This is one of the many things I still love about working in this industry: no two days are the same and being bored isn't much of an option. I quickly began to understand how my work before entering cyber security was relevant – people are easily as central to this discipline as technology.

The history of cyber security

The history of cyber security starts many years before the invention of the computer. Encryption – a system of encoding data to prevent prying eyes from reading it – is often assumed to be so entwined with computers that we can forget that this cornerstone of cyber security is thousands of years old. It is claimed that Histiaeus, a Greek ruler in the 6th century, tattooed a military message on the shaved head of a slave before waiting for the hair to grow back and sending the slave to his ally with a message to remove his hair and read the secret missive.

Julius Caesar is credited with inventing one of the first encoding systems, aptly called the Caesar cipher or Caesar shift. The Caesar cipher is very simple compared to the encryption mechanisms we have in place now, but at the time was revolutionary. It is a substitution cipher in which each plaintext letter of a message is replaced by a letter a fixed number of positions down the alphabet. So, if there is a rotation right 4, A would become E, B would become F and so on. For example, if we are going to encode the words 'shift example' and shift four to the right, it would become 'wlmjx ibeqtpi'. This is illustrated in the wheel below.

Different rotations give different encodings. Try to decode this phrase, which has been encoded using a Caesar cipher (tip: you will need to work out the rotation number first): 'Guvf vf na rknzcyr bs n Pnrfne pvcure. Jryy qbar sbe qrpbqvat vg!'.

The answer is on page 243.

To cover the entire history of cyber security would take a whole book, or even several books – and we don't need to know *absolutely everything* in order to develop in-demand cyber security skills. Table 0.1 provides a quick timeline: this covers some of the key points in the evolution of information security.

0.1

TABLE 0.1   Cyber security timeline

c.50 BC	Julius Caesar creates the Caesar cipher
1903	Nevil Maskelyne breaks into a demonstration of Marconi's wireless telegraphy, to highlight it is not secure and private
1916–18	Enigma cipher machine invented by German engineer Arthur Scherbius. The encryption device is used extensively by Nazi Germany in the Second World War
1932	Polish cryptologists Marian Rejewski, Henryk Zygalski and Jerzy Różycki break the Enigma machine code, enabling the Polish Cipher Bureau to read German Enigma messages from 1933
1939	Alan Turing creates the Bombe computer at Bletchley Park in the UK, developed from a device made by the Polish Cipher Bureau; the Bombe helps decipher German secret messages, encrypted using Enigma during World War II
1943–45	Tommy Flowers designs Colossus, widely regarded as the world's first programmable, electric, digital computer
1949	The paper 'Theory and organization of complicated automata' by John von Neumann outlines self-replication of computer programs
1940s	The American mathematician Norbert Wiener uses the term 'cybernetics' to mean 'control or communication theory, whether in the machine or in the animal'[1]
1955	The word 'hack', to mean messing around with machines, is coined at the MIT Tech Model Railroad Club
1957	Josef Carl Engressia ('joybubbles'), a blind 7-year-old boy with perfect pitch, can whistle 2600 mhz, which is a tone that can control American telephone systems; alongside John Draper, he starts the Phreaking scene

(*continued*)

TABLE 0.1   (Continued)

1961	MIT's Compatible Time-Sharing System (CTSS) requires users to log in with a password; in the 1960s passwords start to be used on other computer systems
1970s	The Advanced Research Projects Agency Network (ARPANET) is invented, a precursor to the internet
1971	Ray Tomlinson is credited with inventing email, after implementing the first email program on ARPANET
1971	Creeper, the first computer virus in history, spreads the message 'I'm the creeper, catch me if you can' over ARPANET computers; the virus is harmless, created by Bob Thomas to test his theory that programs could be moved across computers
1971	Reaper is developed in response to Creeper (it is not known who created it; some claim it was Bob Thomas himself, whilst others credit Ray Tomlinson). Reaper detects Creeper on a computer and deletes it
1972	Rabbit, the first malicious virus, infects computers, reproduces itself and causes the system to crash
1981	*New York Times* reports on hackers and describes ethical hacking activities[2]
1982	The internet protocol suite (TCP/IP) is standardized, which enables worldwide proliferation of interconnected networks. Commercial internet service providers (ISPs) are set up in the late 1980s and early 1990s
1983	Six bills concerning cybercrime introduced in the USA after the activities of the 414s hacking group, the first widely recognized group of hackers
1984	*The Hacker Quarterly* is first published

(*continued*)

TABLE 0.1   (Continued)

1985	Robert Schifreen and Stephen Gold arrested for hacking into a BT computer and accessing TeleCom Gold (an early email system) communications of Prince Philip; in 1986 they are convicted under the Forgery and Counterfeiting Act (the first people to be charged with forgery that deceived a non-human target) due to a lack of contemporary legislation in the UK against computer hacking
1986	Clifford Stoll locates Marcus Hess using a honeypot; Hess had hacked into a network of US, European and East Asian military and industrial computers and sold the information to the KGB[3]
1986	US Congress passes the Computer Fraud and Abuse Act, making breaking into computers a crime
1988	The Morris Worm, written by Robert Morris, is one of the first worms distributed via the internet and spreads to over 6,000 of the approximately 60,000 computers connected to the internet at the time. Robert Morris is the first felony conviction under the US Computer Fraud and Abuse Act[4]
1988	Computer Emergency Response Team (CERT) formed at Carnegie Mellon University
1988	First CERT Advisory issued
1989	Sir Tim Berners-Lee invents the World Wide Web
1990	ARPANET decommissioned
1990	The UK introduces the Computer Misuse Act
Early 1990s	The first firewalls are used
1995	CVSSv1 is launched to rank computer system vulnerabilities (see Chapter 3 for more information)

(continued)

TABLE 0.1   (Continued)

1999	Mitre CVE list created to make it easier to share information on computer system vulnerabilities (see Chapter 3 for more information)
2003	OWASP top 10 first published, with the aim of highlighting information on the most critical computer vulnerabilities
2013	Edward Snowden leaks classified information from the US National Security Agency, revealing global surveillance programmes and techniques
2014	The UK launches its first CERT (CERT-UK)
2017	The UK National Cyber Security Centre is established, as the public-facing arm of GCHQ
2017	Wannacry ransomware spreads globally, with the cryptoworm targeting computers running Microsoft Windows operating system. A security researcher going by the handle MalwareTech stops the spread of the attack
2018	The Cybersecurity and Infrastructure Security Agency (CISA) is established in the United States. CISA's mission is to lead the national effort to understand, manage and reduce risk to cyber and physical infrastructure in the USA
2020	SolarWinds compromise is identified. Subsequently described as 'the largest and most sophisticated attack the world has ever seen' by Microsoft Corp President Brad Smith
2021	The Log4J/Log4Shell vulnerability is discovered and rated a maximum 10 out of 10 CVSS score (see Chapter 3 for more on CVSS)

Cyber security, you and your career

It is important to understand where we have come from, as an industry and a community, to fully appreciate where we are now; so, now that we've finished our potted history, let's go on to explore the different facets of cyber security today, from the technical to the physical and the human considerations. We will look at the different careers available in the industry, and hear from some amazing people working in the field. Hopefully, you will finish the book with an understanding of the complex challenges we face in this field, an appreciation of how diverse the industry is and an awareness of where cyber security applies to you and, perhaps, how you could have a career in this fast-paced, relevant and important profession. Some people love working in cyber security because of the technical challenges they can tackle; others are drawn to it because it is a means by which they can help others. For many of us, it is these reasons and more. One thing most of us in this community have in common is curiosity, and a drive to learn more and solve puzzles. I hope this book satisfies some of your curiosity about cyber security, but I also believe that if reading this book prompts more questions in your mind, and you have the drive to go away and start finding the answers to those questions, that is a pretty solid sign that you have the perfect mindset for a satisfying and successful career in cyber security.

Confidence

Most of this book is about cyber security. The aim is to help readers be confident about all aspects of cyber security, whether you are new to the field, exploring opportunities or simply want to get up to speed on this increasingly important topic. But, I want to spend a little time explicitly exploring the first word in the title. What does it mean to be confident? Can we become more confident – and if so, how? What does confidence mean in relation to the field of cyber security? And, is there a danger of overconfidence?

I've spoken on live, national and international television over a hundred times in the last decade. I've delivered over 80 global keynotes, sometimes to rooms of thousands of people, and to audiences that include government, military, intelligence, and business leaders. I've delivered in-person cyber security awareness-raising sessions to over 50,000 people and countless more online. Most terrifyingly, I have spoken to thousands of teenagers about cyber security.

And yet, when I started all of this, I would never have described myself as confident. My confidence will always remain a work in progress.

I am an introvert who has learned how to operate as an extrovert. A shy person who has overcome public speaking anxiety to become a media commentator and keynote speaker.

Imposter phenomenon

First identified by the psychological research of Imes and Clance in the 1970s, imposter phenomenon (then referred to as imposter syndrome) is generally found among high achievers who find it difficult to internalize their success. People with imposter phenomenon generally attribute their achievements to luck rather than ability and worry that people will eventually discover they are a fraud. Because of this, people often suffer in silence, sometimes accompanied with anxiety and depression.

In their 1970s research, Imes and Clance believed that imposter phenomenon only affected women. There can still be a perception that women suffer from imposter phenomenon more than men. However, recent research suggests this is not the case, and the many conversations I have had with people about imposter syndrome suggest the same: men are just as likely to suffer as women.

Those of us working in cyber security are often driven to achieve. We want to make a difference. We generally hold ourselves to a very high standard; we don't want to fail. And, we are working in a hugely broad field that is also incredibly deep. We cannot know everything about cyber security, and yet, we look at colleagues working in different areas and feel that they know more. We don't consider that they are probably looking at us and thinking the same.

It is important to recognize cultural factors and power dynamics, too. Imposter phenomenon is found to be more prevalent among minority groups.[5] While we strive for greater diversity and inclusion in the cyber security field, we have much progress still to make. Discussions of imposter phenomenon typically point our attention towards the individual. While taking personal responsibility for our own confidence and development is important, we must not neglect the role of environment in fostering confidence and psychological safety:

> Even as we know it today, imposter syndrome puts the blame on individuals, without accounting for the historical and cultural contexts that are foundational to how it manifests in both women of color and white women[6]

Building a culture of cyber security that is inclusive and empowering is very close to my heart. It is fundamental in families, organizations and communities if we want people to engage in learning about security and practising secure behaviours. If we want a diverse and confident workforce within cyber security then we must focus on building an inclusive and empowering culture of security within the community, too. One in which questions are encouraged, not judged, and where collaboration and communication are healthy and respectful. Where bias is addressed, and psychological safety is championed.

A growth mindset

When we believe our talents are fixed, we are more afraid that we may be unmasked, and our shortcomings exposed. In contrast, a growth mindset (one in which we recognize that our abilities can be developed) enables us to take on challenges and be more concerned with learning than with appearing smart. Professor Carol Dweck, Professor of Psychology at Stanford University, coined the terms growth and fixed mindset. She explains that these perceptions of ourselves do not exist as a dichotomy but more of a spectrum, and that we can all operate at different levels on this spectrum at different times and in different contexts. She suggests being observant of 'trigger moments' when we respond with a fixed mindset, for example if we are criticized or if we see someone being more successful in a field that we are good at. Dweck suggests that we can encourage ourselves to embrace more of a growth mindset during these pivotal moments, which is not only more healthy but also more likely to enable us to adapt and succeed.[7]

For me personally, leaning into my love of learning has been pivotal in developing my confidence. One of the reasons I am so committed to cyber security is because there is always something new to learn. One of the main sources of energy in my life is trying new hobbies and learning new skills (over the years I have taken lessons in piano, guitar, ballroom dancing, fencing, piloting a plane, circus skills, ceramics, singing and horse riding). Trying new things helps me embrace new challenges, persist with skills which do not come naturally to me and love the progress of getting better. This mindset also helps me embrace learning opportunities in my professional life, rather than succumb to the (often self-imposed) expectation that I must know everything. Developing a growth mindset helps you focus more on the process rather than perfection, which is inherent in cyber security, and which will make you a more successful and resilient professional.

Dweck also explores what this means at the organizational level, addressing the way in which some organizations worship fixed talent whereas others champion the approach that everyone can develop their abilities. Employees in growth mindset organizations reported feeling more empowered and committed to that organization.[8] It is not a stretch to apply this to cyber security. When we take an approach that values people and their ability to develop security skills (whether in a professional sense or a more day-to-day setting), we set them – and us – up for success.

Stress, burnout and mental health

It is widely acknowledged that pushing yourself out of your comfort zone enables growth. The often-posted quote 'a comfort zone is a beautiful place, but nothing grows there' is generally accepted without challenge. However, it should come with a warning, because constantly operating outside of your comfort zone can contribute to stress, burnout and further mental health challenges.

I do believe in stretching my comfort zone. It has been helpful to my confidence, at work and beyond. But I also believe in protecting mental health above all else. Knowing when to fight the complacency of a comfort zone, and when to guard its boundaries, is an important foundation for confidence.

Working in cyber security can be high-stress and it can feel thankless. The work of cyber security professionals is often invisible – until something goes wrong. The threat landscape feels like it is constantly growing, and the pace of technological change is swift. Attaining leadership support (and funding) can be a challenge and many teams are under-resourced. Responding to incidents can be physically and mentally draining. Inevitably, we are often focused on flaws, on negatives, on being hyper-vigilant.

The cyber security company Sekuro surveyed 101 cyber security professionals in 2022 and found that 91 per cent had experienced mental health challenges at work in the two previous years. Fifty-one per cent attributed their mental health challenges to their work environment (poor culture and management styles) and 50 per cent cited the high-stress nature of the job.[9]

Thankfully, the cyber security community has become more aware of the mental health challenges we can all face. In a survey of over 1,000 cyber security professionals, the security automation company Tines found that 57 per cent had workplaces which provide resources and support for mental well-being.[10]

Overconfidence

Confidence is an asset, but overconfidence is risky. The more we know about a topic, the more we feel safe in that knowledge, which means we can easily be lulled into a false sense of security:

> the better protected you are and the less likely you think you'll
> be a victim, the more you're apt to lose if a con artist can find a
> way to earn your trust. It ends up that the more you know about
> something, the more likely you are to fall for a con in that specific
> area.[11]

Illusory superiority (also known as superiority bias and the Lake Wobegon effect) is a cognitive bias whereby we overestimate our intelligence and ability compared with others. We think we are better than everyone else. When it comes to cyber security, it can be easy to think that because we have knowledge of cybercrime and scams, we are better than those who lack such knowledge and that we are resistant to cyber attacks and social engineering – but this is highly misleading. For example, research suggests that how confident we feel identifying phishing emails has no bearing on whether we can, in fact, successfully identify phishing.[12]

I don't share this to suggest that you stop reading now or that you embrace the anxiety of imposter syndrome. I simply want to remind us all that, while knowledge and confidence are valuable, an illusion of superiority and immunity inevitably makes us more vulnerable.

Notes

1 Wiener, N (1961) *Cybernetics: Or control and communication in the animal and the machine*, MIT Press.
2 www.nytimes.com/1981/07/26/business/case-of-the-purloined-password.html (archived at https://perma.cc/QYK4-GY8T)
3 Stoll, C (2007) *The Cuckoo's Egg: Tracking a spy through the maze of computer espionage*, Gallery Books.
4 www.fbi.gov/news/stories/morris-worm-30-years-since-first-major-attack-on-internet-110218. (archived at https://perma.cc/Q44R-24WJ)
5 https://www.apa.org/gradpsych/2013/11/fraud (archived at https://perma.cc/HRN2-E86X)
6 https://hbr.org/2021/02/stop-telling-women-they-have-imposter-syndrome (archived at https://perma.cc/GL63-89H6)
7 https://youtu.be/-71zdXCMU6A (archived at https://perma.cc/E2MD-FFGN)
8 Dweck, C (2007) *Mindset: The new psychology of success*, Ballantine Books, New York
9 Sekuro Cyber Security Mental Health Survey. https://sekuro.io/cyber-mental-health (archived at https://perma.cc/5ZM8-N2NA)
10 https://www.tines.com/reports/state-of-mental-health-in-cybersecurity (archived at https://perma.cc/T96D-A4KK)
11 Konnikova, M (2016) *The Confidence Game: The psychology of the con and why we fall for it*, Canongate Books, Edinburgh
12 Wang, Jingguo; Li, Yuan; and Rao, H. Raghav (2016) 'Overconfidence in Phishing Email Detection,' *Journal of the Association for Information Systems*, 17(11), . DOI: 10.17705/1jais.00442 Available at: https://aisel.aisnet.org/jais/vol17/iss11/1 (archived at https://perma.cc/2NMJ-U2NT)

PART ONE

Why cyber security?

CHAPTER ONE

What cyber security is

Cyber security has technically only been around for a few decades, yet it is now so mainstream that it's in the dictionary, defined as:

> Measures taken to protect a computer or computer system (as on the internet) against unauthorized access or attack.

Whilst the dictionary defines protection of *computers* as central to cyber security, I would argue that it is more precisely about protecting *information*. We're not protecting the computers, but what is on the computers (for example, confidential plans for a new product); what the computers provide access to (for example, your online banking); or what the computers are programmed to do (for example, operate power plants).

At first glance, then, cyber security might sound inherently and absolutely technical. This is certainly the popular image: a green screen of code, geeks in hoodies, blinking lights and neon streams of light. The reality is that, whilst technology is of course central to cyber security, the discipline is much wider than that.

The types of jobs in the profession vary widely, from deeply technical to very much people-focused.

Here's why: technology does not exist in a vacuum. Technology is invented and developed by humans. Code is written by people – people who inadvertently create bugs that make technology vulnerable. People then interact with technology, and use it in ways it was not intended to be used. Then there's the physical aspect: technology, of course, has a physical as well as digital presence. Data is stored in servers, which are in turn located in warehouses; computers (whether desktop, laptop or smartphones) sit unattended in offices and coffee shops, and are prone to being lost and stolen. Criminals seek to profit from these vulnerabilities, with their human motivations and methods. Understanding the intricacies of all of these factors, and how they interplay with one another, takes people with expertise and skill in all of the different areas spanning digital, human and physical. Cyber attacks and data breaches are always the result of human, technical or physical issues (or a combination of all three) and so, to properly defend individuals, organizations and countries, we need expertise in all of these areas.

The cyber security rainbow: Red, blue and purple

There are many, many different specialisms in cyber security and, like most professions, these are wrapped in jargon. There's a lot of colour in the terminology: we'll start by looking at the red, blue and purple teams. (You may find that some people will argue that the definitions of red, blue and purple team should be much more narrow than the following, but for the purposes of understanding the different roles in this industry, and how they can be grouped together to perform different functions, we will use a wider definition.)

Those who simulate attacks on organizations are called the *red team*. They 'break in' to companies, under a legal agreement with that company, in order to identify vulnerabilities, which can then be fixed before cyber criminals exploit them. Red teamers are sometimes employed directly, but they are most commonly from specialist companies, or individuals working as freelancers, who are engaged by organizations as and when they want a test.

The red team is testing the defences put in place by the *blue team*. The blue team work to protect companies from cyber criminals, and these protections are tested by red teamers to see if they can bypass them (which would mean that criminals could). Just like the red team, blue teamers can be employed directly by a company or can be brought in from specialist companies to do distinct pieces of work. In the best scenario, the red and blue teams work closely to ensure that the defences are as robust as they can be.

If the team is blended, or an individual has skills across both attack and defence, they are commonly known as purple (because when red and blue paint is mixed, it makes purple). However, the *purple team* might not be a purple person, or even a team made up of red people and blue people: it can also be understood as a concept, or a way of working within an organization, in which the red and blue teams work very collaboratively to ensure that the organization is as secure as possible.

Within the red, blue and purple teams are specialisms that draw on technical, human or physical skills (or a combination of them).

The red team

In the red team, people whose jobs centre on simulating attacks on organizations, there are *social engineers*. We'll cover social engineering in Chapters 4 and 5, so won't go into detail here, but ethical social engineers are hired to 'break into' organizations, which can be physically, digitally or via the people working there. Organizations don't generally have social engineers on the payroll; rather, they may have people who work on their red team with social engineering skills or they will hire people to carry out social engineering assessments of the organization from time to time. Given the nature of their role, these individuals may have skills that span human, physical and technical domains (or are focused on one of the three). Social engineers may break in physically to organizations, or they may social engineer their way in (for example, talking their way past the receptionist, or making a phone call to someone in the company and masquerading as someone else as a way of getting information out of them). They may send a *spear-phishing* email or text, just like criminals, as a way of getting the credentials of someone in the company and accessing their systems (we'll look more at spear-phishing in Chapter 5).[1] Once in the building or on the network, they may use technical skills to compromise the information technology (IT) systems further; for example, if they broke into the building physically, they may plant a rogue access point that people in the company will then unwittingly use to connect to the internet and expose their data.

Also on the red team are *penetration testers* ('pen testers'), otherwise known as ethical hackers. Pen testers work on behalf of the organization, with their legal consent, to break into the computer systems. They will work to a scope and often use a number of tools: for example, Kali Linux, Wireshark, the SE Toolkit and John the Ripper. They identify vulnerabilities in the systems and report these back to the organization, with recommended mitigations. Over the last 10 to 15 years there has been a rise in bug bounties, which are schemes run by organizations (sometimes via a bug bounty platform) to offer rewards to anyone who identifies a vulnerability in their system. Again, the organization is usually very specific about which parts of their systems are under a bug bounty and, of course, not all companies engage in bug bounties. It probably should go without saying, but let's say it explicitly anyway: *you should not test a company's security without their explicit permission and a*

22

signed contract, unless what you are doing falls under a bug bounty. If you challenge or test a company's cyber security without a contract or outside of a bug bounty, you are not performing a pen test, you are illegally hacking them!

The blue team

On the blue team, there are many roles. Attackers need to find just one flaw in an organization's security to compromise it, or at least to begin compromising it, so they really just need to win once. Defenders need to make sure everything in the company, from the people to the physical measures to the technical systems, has an adequate level of security. Defenders need to win 100 per cent of the time.

Most large organizations have a chief information security officer (CISO), who sets the strategy, decides where the budget should be spent and ultimately takes responsibility for security within that organization. They lead the security team. Every organization is different: some will have a large security team, some a small one, and some will have no internal security teams at all.

One role that has become more common in recent years is people working on the human side of cyber security, which can take the form of people working on raising awareness of cyber security within the organization, and getting the culture right. This involves ensuring that people understand why security is important, what threats are relevant to the company and what they need to do to play their part in keeping the company as secure as possible. More and more organizations have people working on this internally, as well as bringing in specialists to support them. This is what I have specialized in during my career in cyber security: understanding what a good cyber security culture looks like, how to engender that culture and raising awareness.

Many roles in security are not internal ones, with people working for just one company. As many security professionals have specialist skills, they will often work for a security company or as a freelancer, and then large companies will hire them as and when they need their skills. This can include:

- reverse engineers, who unpick a technology to find vulnerabilities in it, and malware reverse engineers who take malicious software (malware) and understand how it works;
- specialists in investigations, who work out what has happened after a company is hit by a cyber attack and potentially who was behind it. This includes forensic specialists who recover data from computer systems where there has been an intrusion and work to piece together the details of what happened;
- incident response professionals who help an organization continue operating when a cyber attack is underway or has just occurred, and help them recover from any damage that was inflicted.

The cyber security spectrum: Who are the hackers?

The term 'hacker' *can* be understood in lots of different ways. As we covered in the introduction, the term 'hack' was coined to mean messing around with machines. For many people today, the label hacker is seen as synonymous with 'criminal', but there are plenty of people who hack legally and ethically.

Hackers

The pen testers we referred to earlier are hackers, often called ethical hackers. If they should be called anything beyond 'hacker', it would probably be more precise to call them legal hackers (because saying they are ethical does not necessarily confirm that they are also operating legally). I'm going to generally call them hackers, and when they are not legal/ethical hackers, I will call them criminals or cyber criminals.

Hackers use the same tools and techniques as cyber criminals, but there is an important fundamental difference: hackers do so within the boundaries of the law. Hackers operate within a scope and contract, hacking an organization with that organization's permission, to identify vulnerabilities and suggest mitigations to enable the organization to fix them (or at least, to be aware of them), and to prevent the criminals from exploiting them. Hackers often work as penetration testers (see below) and can be employed by the company directly, particularly if the company is large, or work for specialist cyber security companies or operate freelance. Hackers are in incredibly trusted roles and good intentions are not enough: you may want to test the defences of an organization, website or application for the right reasons, but without an agreement from the organization itself, you are in uncertain territory, at the least. If you carry out such a hack without permission, you will probably find that you are no longer a hacker, you are a criminal.

Criminals

Criminal hackers are at the opposite end of the scale to ethical or legal hackers; these are people who carry out illegal hacking activity to circumvent the access controls of organizations. We'll look in more detail at cybercrime, and cyber criminals, later in this chapter (and, indeed, throughout the book).

Grey hat hackers

It should be simple, shouldn't it? You're either a hacker or a criminal. But, of course, little in security is simple. Let's say someone hacks a website for the right reasons (to identify vulnerabilities before criminals get to them) but without the agreement of the website owner: then this fits into the category of grey hat hacking. Grey hat hackers, as the name suggests, sit in a murky area of the law. Grey hat hackers may have good intentions, as in the example above, but without the legal permission to carry out those intentions, they end up actually breaking the law. Another way a hacker might be defined as grey is to be hired as a legitimate hacker but go out-of-scope, beyond what has been agreed – again, this may be with good intentions (to ultimately make the organization more secure, not to profit from a vulnerability themselves), but by straying out of the scope of the legal agreement, they stray into grey hat territory.

The term grey hat comes from a tradition of using black hat to refer to criminal hackers and white hat to refer to legal / ethical hackers (with grey hats somewhere in the middle). This itself came from black and white cowboy films in which the hero would often wear a white hat, and the villain a black hat, as a visual cue for viewers. However, it is increasingly recognized as inappropriate to use terminology which implies that black equals bad and white equals good, so I have not used the terms white hat and black hat, especially as the words *hacker* and *criminal* bring more clarity anyway. However, I have used grey hat, because I believe it works as a standalone term (alluding to a grey area of the law) and a replacement term has not (yet) emerged.

Hacking and the law

Despite the apparently stark boundaries implied by the labels criminal hacker, legal hacker and grey hat hacker, in real life it's often not that simple. Legislation of cyber security, and cyber *in*security, is a challenge.

The field moves quickly, but legislation moves slowly – and those in charge of the law are not always best informed of the latest intricacies of cyber security. On top of this, legislation is very geographically defined, with different countries taking very different approaches to legislating cybercrime and security research. Of course, cyberspace doesn't have physical boundaries in the same sense as countries and legislation: someone can be in one country hacking someone in another and routing their activity through countless more. What one country recognizes as legitimate hacking, another may see as criminal activity. Where one country will penalize cybercrime very heavily, regardless of the intention of the hacker, others will consider whether the individual actually meant to cause harm. Because of this, legal, criminal and grey hat hacking could be better understood as activities rather than roles. It's more than possible for someone to start as a legal hacker, step outside the boundaries of their legal agreement with an organization and move into grey hat hacking, before deciding that they actually want to take advantage of their insider information and, for example, sell the vulnerabilities they have discovered on the dark web, thus becoming criminal.

Cybercrime

Criminal hackers can be split into different groups according to their motivations and methods. This is important to understand, as different groups will target different people and companies. Organizations have the best chance of defending themselves when they understand which group or groups are likely to attack them and why, as that means they can target their defences.

Financially motivated cybercrime

A large bulk of cybercrime on the internet is financially motivated. Organized criminal gangs – people who have always operated in crime – now understand that carrying out criminal activity online is easier, faster, cheaper, less risky and more likely to be successful than crime in the 'real world'. Financially motivated cyber criminals want money and they will attempt to get it by coercing it out of companies or people; for example, by getting access to their bank accounts or pretending to be a supplier needing a transfer of money to a new bank account. Cybercrime as a service facilitates this: on the dark web, criminal hackers can be hired to perform an attack on a company and malware can be purchased with instructions on how to deploy it. Other financially motivated criminal operations will run like other big, legitimate companies, hiring people to work in-house on attacking targets, even with different departments such as 'customer support'.

Financially motivated cyber criminals target all organizations, not just large corporations – and, in fact, not all financially motivated cybercrime is targeted. The rise in ransomware, for example, has seen a huge number of smaller companies and sole traders fall victim to financially motivated cybercrime, as well as non-commercial organizations such as charities, universities and hospitals.

Script kiddies

Many of the people that financially motivated criminal gangs have working for them would not be classed as hackers, but as *script kiddies*. Script kiddies are individuals who do not have a great deal of hacking knowledge or skill, but are able to use other people's code and pre-built tools to perform attacks on organizations. There are many tools freely available, many of which have been built for pen testing purposes, that are used by script kiddies. There are also videos on platforms such as YouTube that will show people, step by step, how to hack without them needing to understand what they are doing. So, financially motivated criminal operators will hire script kiddies to work for them – but script kiddies also carry out attacks on organizations under their own steam.

CASE STUDY   Lapsus$

Research suggests that most script kiddies are motivated by the desire to tackle a technical problem and show off to their friends.[2] However, this does not mean that they are not also motivated by money. In 2022, the Lapsus$ group quickly gained notoriety for their cyber-extortion activities. They are attributed with compromising Microsoft, Uber, Okta, Nvidia, Samsung, and Brazil's Ministry of Health. The City of London Police began leading an international investigation into the gang and the FBI launched an appeal for information on Lapsus$ members. The City of London Police arrested seven people in the UK in connection with their investigation, all aged between 16 and 21. As news of the arrests became public, Lapsus$ shared with its 45,000 followers on Telegram that some of its members were taking 'a vacation'. One of those arrested, a 16 year old from Oxford, was understood to be one of the leaders of the gang and allegedly amassed £10.6 million.[3]

Hacktivists

Hacking is not always motivated by financial gain. This is the case with *hacktivists*, or online activists who are motivated by political, ideological or ethical reasons to attack a company. The most well-known activist group is probably Anonymous, the collective of hacktivists who carried out a large number of attacks on companies and organizations, particularly in 2011. IBM found a 95 per cent drop in hacktivist attacks from 2015 to 2018, alongside a decline in the number of attacks carried out by the Anonymous collective and associated groups.[4]

Nation-state hackers

Over the last few years, we have heard more about one type of hacking group than ever before: nation-state hackers. There is often talk in cyber security of the *advanced persistent threat* (*APT*) – which refers to the level of sophistication that can be achieved by nation-state hackers; they have the budget, time, resources, motivation and skill to pursue a target until they have compromised it. The truth is that most cybercrime does not fall under this umbrella; most cybercrime is not carried out by sophisticated nation-state hackers, but rather is low-skill criminal activity that compromises known vulnerabilities or exploits people. Most people, most organizations, are not targeted by nation states (however, they can sometimes be caught up in collateral damage).

When a nation state *does* seek to compromise a target, they will start with the same methods as any other cyber criminal: known vulnerabilities and social engineering. But after this is where financially motivated cyber criminals and nation-state actors differ: if a financially motivated cyber criminal targets a company and fails, they will most likely move on to the next target. However, if a nation-state actor targets an organization and fails, they will usually move on to more sophisticated methods of compromise. Having a good level of security is an excellent defence for most cybercrime, and will protect against a lot of criminal endeavours, but protecting against a determined nation-state attack is very, very difficult. Luckily, this is not within the threat model of most individuals or organizations.

Cygenta's work with organizations that have been victims of cybercrime is the basis of the bell curve shown in Figure 1.1, which reflects that the large proportion of cybercrime is conducted by financially motivated criminal gangs and script kiddies (although of course it differs depending on the organization). The reference to McArthur Wheeler alludes to criminals that are so lacking in skill and knowledge they are not a concern, because they essentially catch themselves. McArthur Wheeler is the case of a man who was arrested in 1995 when he robbed two banks in Pittsburgh, the United States, after being identified on CCTV. He had covered himself in lemon juice after reading that it could be used as invisible ink, and reaching the conclusion that

FIGURE 1.1   Cybercrime bell curve

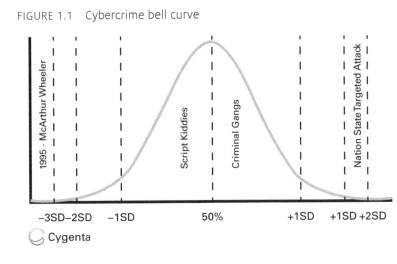

Cygenta

it would therefore make *him* invisible on video cameras. Incidentally, the McArthur Wheeler case was the inspiration for psychologists David Dunning and Justin Kruger to conduct research that confirmed the cognitive bias in which some people inflate their cognitive ability (widely known as the Dunning-Kruger effect).

CASE STUDY   Evil Corp

On the surface, ransomware could be considered a financially motivated crime. Criminals compromise an organization (sometimes through technical means; often via social engineering) and use malicious software (malware) to encrypt their data or their network. They then hold the data to ransom, promising that they will make it available to the organization once again, if their fee is paid. It is now common for the criminals not just to prevent their victims from accessing their data, but also to threaten to leak sensitive data if the ransom is not paid. The UK NCSC describe ransomware as 'the most acute threat that businesses and organizations in the UK face' and consider it a national security risk.[5]

Evil Corp represent the way in which ransomware is not merely a financially motivated crime. The United States Health Sector Cybersecurity Coordination Centre (HC3) describes Evil Corp as 'one of the most capable cybercriminal syndicates in the world', attributing them with creating and operating some of the most powerful malware and ransomware variants in the world. In 2019, the FBI accused nine members of Evil Corp of stealing or extorting over $100 million in hacks that affected over 40 countries. At the same time, the US Justice Department offered a $5 million bounty for information leading to the arrest and conviction of the man accused of leading Evil Corp, Maksim Yakubets, aka aqua. Operating since 2009, Evil Corp is based out of Russia and there is evidence that Russia does not merely turn a blind eye to the criminal group, but that there are deep ties between the two. When the United States Treasury Department's Office of Foreign Assets Control (OFAC) announced sanctions against Evil Corp in 2019, their statement confirmed:

Today's action clarifies that, in addition to his involvement in financially motivated cybercrime, the group's leader, Maksim Yakubets, also provides direct assistance to the Russian government's malicious cyber efforts, highlighting the Russian government's enlistment of cybercriminals for its own malicious purposes.[6]

Evil Corp are an interesting example of the blurring lines between the motivations – and activities – of cyber criminals.
The cyber heist on the Bank of Bangladesh in 2016 is another such example, in which US $80 million was stolen as part of an attempt to steal US $1 billion. On the surface, this attack appears to have been purely financially motivated. However, allegations from the United States suggest otherwise. The US Justice Department has charged a North Korean man, Park Jin Hyok, with involvement in the North Korean Government-sponsored hacking team known as 'Lazarus Group', which they accuse of being responsible not just for the Bank of Bangladesh attack but also others including the 2017 WannaCry 2.0 global ransomware attack and the 2014 hit on Sony Pictures Entertainment,[7] which North Korea denies.[8]

Malicious and non-malicious insiders

So far, we've covered the external threats that organizations might face. However, this of course is not the full picture and, when we look at insiders in an organization, there are two groups we need to consider: malicious and non-malicious insiders.

Malicious insiders

Malicious insiders make the headlines. Malicious insiders usually form one of two types: people who take a role at an organization with the intent to steal (money or information) from that organization; and, more common, people who have usually been at an organization a long time and who have been loyal to the organization until they feel disgruntled and then, feeling like a victim more than a criminal, take revenge on the organization or help themselves to what they believe they deserve as a means of righting the perceived wrong.

Those who take a role with the intentional purpose to steal may be motivated by political reasons, financial reasons or, in certain organizations, because they are working as part of a nation-state group. It has been argued that Edward Snowden fits this profile; that he was a spy for Russia or China (or even both) and took the role as a contractor for the US National Security Agency with the intentional purpose of stealing information, some of which he then released to the public via WikiLeaks.[9]

More common than those who take roles in an organization with the express purpose of accessing and stealing data are those who turn into malicious insiders. Malicious insiders who fall into this category usually do not feel that they are the ones in the wrong. They feel slighted by the organization that they may have spent many years working loyally for. There will usually be an external pressure on these individuals: perhaps they have debts, their spouse has been made redundant or they have family problems. Often, they have not received a promotion or bonus that they feel they deserve; they feel their hard work goes unrecognized and unrewarded; or they have been disciplined for something and resent this, feeling it is unfair.

CASE STUDY   Apple Inc v Rivos Inc

In April 2022, Apple filed a lawsuit against technology startup Rivos Inc, bringing the action 'to prevent Rivos and its employees from exploiting Apple's most valuable trade secrets to compete with Apple unlawfully and unfairly'.[10] Apple claim that Rivos hired over 40 of its former employees to work on competing system-on-chip (SoC) technology and that at least two former Apple engineers took gigabytes of confidential information with them to Rivos. The lawsuit also claims that several other former Apple employees took confidential documents when they left Apple to work at Rivos.

Apple claims that the employees transferred sensitive SoC specifications and design files to their personal devices using USB devices, AirDrop, personal Google Drive folders and that one even made a full Time Machine backup of their entire corporate Apple device, saving it to a personal external hard drive. Furthermore, Apple claims that they believe their former employees were instructed to download and install apps for encrypted communications with Rivos (specifically referring to the Signal app). Apple is suggesting that this is a case of coordinated corporate espionage orchestrated by Rivos to gain competitive advantage over Apple. This case highlights the challenges that organizations face when trying to keep confidential information under wraps, especially when the lines between personal and corporate devices is blurred and cloud connectivity so widespread. However, the detail of the lawsuit also shows the extent to which many companies can – and do – monitor and log how their employees handle corporate data. It may not always stop such data walking out of the door, but it can paint a picture of how that data was handled before it left the ecosystem.

Malicious insiders can be very costly for organizations. Insiders with the intent to cause harm have knowledge that facilitates their activity; perhaps knowing which data is most valuable, ways to access it, how to cover their tracks and what to do with the data to cause damage. Malicious insiders are also attention-grabbing. When a malicious insider case becomes public, it usually gets a lot of news coverage, especially when it comes with a human story: the disgruntled employee under financial pressure at home, for example. However, far more common than malicious insider activity is non-malicious insider activity.

Non-malicious insiders

Non-malicious insiders are people with good intentions working in organizations. Most people come to work with the intention of doing their job well, or at least not doing harm to the organization they work for. However, for many reasons, people often unwittingly expose data throughout the course of their work. This can be as simple as sending an email of sensitive information and making a mistake with the email address, so that it goes to the wrong person; or sending an email to a large group of people in different organizations and putting their email addresses in the 'to' field of the email, exposing the email addresses to everyone on the list, rather than in the 'bcc' field, which would keep the email addresses confidential.

In the last few years, one of the most common threats to organizations takes advantage of non-malicious insider activity: cyber criminals socially engineering non-malicious insiders. In the ClubCISO Live Vote of 2020, 100 chief information security officers were asked to categorize the cause of material data breaches that had occurred in their organization in the previous 12 months: 40 per cent said malicious cyber criminals and 42 per cent said non-malicious insiders.[11] It is no coincidence that these two numbers are so aligned: many cyber attacks carried out by malicious external actors take advantage of non-malicious insiders.

Non-malicious insider activity includes people being duped by the kind of scams we see in spear-phishing emails, but there are many other instances beyond this. It can be someone misconfiguring a firewall so that the network defences of an organization are not as strong as they could be; a developer who stores personal data in an Amazon web server but leaves access open to the internet rather than locking it down; an administrator who sets the username and password to their server as 'admin' and 'admin'; and individuals using weak passwords, which they re-use elsewhere because the burden of creating and remembering strong, unique passwords for each online account is too great without the use of a password manager.

CASE STUDY   The City of Dallas

In April 2021, the City of Dallas discovered that over 20 terabytes of City information had been lost and was ultimately found to be irretrievable (a total of 8.26 million individual files). This happened in two events during March 2021 and most of the data related to the Dallas Police Department.

An external report, delivered by Kirkland & Ellis LLP in February 2022, concluded that the data loss was caused by a series of actions by an IT technician employed by the City. The data was being moved from cloud storage to on-premises servers due to escalating costs. In attempting to move the data, it was not correctly copied or backed-up before being deleted. The investigation concluded that the technician did not act maliciously, but rather made mistakes due to a lack of training. The report also highlighted the need for better processes and procedures for data migration, and better coordination between City stakeholders. Finally, it was concluded that the City did not identify the incident as critical at the time and did not activate their incident response plan, which would have facilitated a more thorough initial assessment of the issue and greater communication between stakeholders.

This case highlights the importance of training and support for those handling data and the need to have – and use – a comprehensive incident response plan. Through training and support, we can minimize the number and impact of incidents; with active incident response planning, we can respond fully to incidents when they do occur.

EXERCISE 1.1 Assessing the risks

Consider the following organizations and which cyber criminal groups you think would be most likely to target them. Think about the kind of information they handle, who would benefit from accessing that information, or who would like to cause damage to that organization because of the kind of work that they do:

- a multinational bank;
- a political party;
- a local estate agent.

Find some suggested answers in the Appendix.

Notes

1 Spear-phishing is a form of social engineering: fraudulent messages are sent by criminals to their targets, appearing to be from a trusted source, such as the target's friend, boss or bank. Spear-phishing messages will usually play on your emotions to entice you into opening an attachment, sharing your login credentials or clicking a link. Spear-phishing differs from phishing because it is targeted, and this makes it more likely to be successful.

2 Weaver, M (2017) Teenage hackers motivated by morality not money, study finds, *Guardian*, 21 April, www.theguardian.com/society/2017/apr/21/ teenage-hackers-motivated-moral-crusade-money-cybercrime (archived at https://perma.cc/MRK2-38CQ)

3 https://www.bbc.co.uk/news/technology-60864283 (archived at https://perma.cc/VX5Z-JDWG)

4 IBM (2019) IBM X-Force Threat Intelligence Index Report, www.ibm.com/security/data-breach/threat-intelligence (archived at https://perma.cc/VZ4Y-LCL3)

5 https://www.ncsc.gov.uk/files/NCSC-Annual-Review-2022.pdf (archived at https://perma.cc/773R-KEUS)

6 https://home.treasury.gov/news/press-releases/sm845 (archived at https://perma.cc/N322-Y3XS)

7 United States District Court for the Central District of California (2018) Criminal complaint, 8 June, www.justice.gov/usao-cdca/press-release/file/1091951/download (archived at https://perma.cc/3RTA-8FJS)

8 Corkery, M and Goldstein, M (2017) North Korea said to be target of inquiry over $81 million cyberheist, *New York Times*, 22 March, www.nytimes.com/2017/03/22/business/dealbook/north-korea-said-to-be-target-of-inquiry-over-81-million-cyberheist.html?_r=0 (archived at https://perma.cc/X248-6GJC)

9 Epstein, EJ (2017) *How America Lost its Secrets: Edward Snowden, the man and the theft*, Knopf, New York

10 https://fingfx.thomsonreuters.com (archived at https://perma.cc/6W4N-CGCV)

11 ClubCISO (2020) Information Security Maturity Report 2020: Full survey results, www.clubciso.org/downloads (archived at https://perma.cc/G2KM-MTSP)

CHAPTER TWO

Why cyber security is important

Now that we know what cyber security is – why does it matter? Connected information is at the heart of so much: in our personal lives, our work lives and our society as a whole. The internet has grown phenomenally since its invention only a few decades ago. It has become a fundamental part of how we interact at a personal level (everything from social media to online banking), how organizations are run (from instant messaging, email and video conference calls around the world to outsourced online payroll systems, ecommerce sites and much more), and how our critical national infrastructure is managed.

In 2019, over 1.9 billion users logged in to YouTube every month[1] and Facebook estimated that approximately 2.2 billion people were using their 'family' of services (Facebook, WhatsApp, Instagram or Messenger) every day.[2] The top five most valuable brands in the world are technology brands for which connected technology is a fundamental part of their products and services – Apple, Google, Microsoft, Amazon and Facebook.[3] This technology, and the information that is integrated in it, needs protecting from those who seek to abuse it or neglect to protect it. This is why the World Economic Forum recognizes cyber security issues as one of the top five global risks.[4] Cyber security, therefore, seeks to keep us safe at personal, organizational and socio-economic levels.

Information is an asset; in many cases, it is the most valuable asset that organizations have. Information *is* money. The first step in cyber security is to understand those information assets; for example, in a company, which information assets are critical to the running of the company and which would be most sought-after by threat actors? These information assets could include intellectual property, client lists, market strategies and the personnel files of employees. Once the assets have been identified and categorized, it is then important to understand the risks, threats and vulnerabilities associated with them.

Risks, threats and vulnerabilities

Cyber security seeks to keep us safe and secure by managing the risks, threats and vulnerabilities that are inherent in how we interact with information and technology. What do we mean by risks, threats and vulnerabilities? These terms are often mistakenly used interchangeably, but understanding their meanings and how they relate to cyber security is helpful, because managing these factors is what makes cyber security so important.

Risk is the possibility that something bad will happen.
Threat is the bad thing that may happen.
Vulnerability is the weakness that the threat takes advantage of.

So, to put it in a sentence: *risk* is the potential for damage that occurs if a *threat* takes advantage of a *vulnerability* and is realized.

Mosquitos seem to really like to bite me, so I often run the risk of being bitten by mosquitos. The mosquitos are the threat – specifically, them biting me. To use language that you will often hear in cyber security, mosquitos are the *threat actors*. The vulnerability is my skin, which does not offer much defence in the face of a mosquito proboscis.

Risk assessment and management

All risks are not equal, and *risk assessment* is the practice of breaking down risks so we can work towards managing them. We do this by looking at our risks and determining how bad they are, which comes down to how likely they are to happen and what the impact would be if they were realized. This is simplistic, of course, but it's a good way to begin managing risk.

If we return to the mosquito example, I can assess my risk of being bitten by a mosquito and then act accordingly, for example, by reducing the risk or accepting it. I can assess the likelihood of the risk being realized – me getting bitten by a mosquito – by considering factors such as which country I am in and if the weather is humid, to what extent I am near open water, what time of day it is and what clothes I am wearing. I can then think about the impact of the risk being realized. For me, the common impact is that I will have red, itchy marks for a while, and they will irritate me. Sometimes, I react more strongly, and the bites swell up. Of course, mosquitos can carry diseases, and this risk is certainly more serious than simply being irritated. I can look at all of these likelihood and impact factors surrounding the risk (where I am, whether mosquitos in that area are likely to carry infectious diseases, my personal reaction to mosquito bites, etc) and then decide what to do about the risk: accept it, or seek to mitigate it.

Mitigations are what we put in place to minimize the likelihood or impact of a threat, for example by patching a vulnerability. In the mosquito example, mitigations include staying indoors with windows and doors shut, burning citronella candles, using anti-mosquito products, wearing light-coloured clothing and taking anti-malaria tablets.

Mitigations can be effective in stopping a risk from being realized, by protecting or fixing a vulnerability and blocking the threat. However, sometimes they are not enough. I could use all of the mitigations above and still get bitten by a mosquito. Therefore, we need to consider not just how to avoid risks, but also how to respond to them if they are realized: these responses range from reactive to proactive. We can return to assessing likelihood and impact to determine how we plan our responses: in the mosquito example, this could range from having a stock of products to alleviate the irritation of a bite to having inoculations and taking anti-malaria tablets while travelling. We can decide which mitigations to put in place according to how likely we believe it is that the threat will be realized, and what the impact would be if it were. The products to alleviate irritation are reactive responses and the inoculations and anti-malaria tablets are proactive responses.

As humans, we live with risk all the time, and having a proportionate approach to risk helps us live our lives while minimizing the likelihood and impact of bad things happening. Some risks can be managed to such an extent that they disappear, or are no longer relevant to us, but risk in general is something we have to live with. Returning to our mosquito example for one last time, we could bathe in anti-mosquito products, refuse to ever leave the house and clothe our bodies from head to toe, in an attempt to manage the risk, but doing this would be to the detriment of our lives (and we still wouldn't completely remove the risk). We need to balance mitigating risks with enabling our lives. The same is true of information and cyber security: we need to balance using technology with managing the risks that are associated with that use.

When we create, share, store or delete information, we run the risk of it being accessed or used in a way that is damaging to us. This has always been the case, but it has heightened with the growth of the internet – there is more information, it is more connected and it is more frequently exposed to more vulnerabilities. Arguably, there are more threat actors – certainly threat actors have realized that the growth of the internet is an opportunity for them.

RISK, THREAT, VULNERABILITY AND MITIGATIONS

Let's look at an example of risk, threat, vulnerability and mitigations in terms of cyber security.

You're building a website, so you are running the *risk* of it being hacked when it goes live. The *threat* is the website being compromised and taken offline, defaced or information being stolen. The likelihood and impact of these threats occurring, and the risks being realized, vary depending upon factors including the sort of site you are running and the information you will be holding. There are many *vulnerabilities*, including authentication, hosting and coding flaws. You *mitigate* these by setting a strong, unique password and using multi-factor authentication; using a reputable hosting company that has firewalls and other protective mechanisms rather than hosting it yourself; and assessing the hosting company's policies and practices to ensure they have an adequate level of security in place and that the software in use is updated.

Cyber security is essentially all about managing the risks, threats and vulnerabilities that organizations face by understanding them, mitigating them where possible (or consciously accepting them) and planning responses if the mitigations fail. Throughout this book, there are many case studies, scenarios and examples that will include threats, vulnerabilities, mitigations and responses. It is important to recognize that vulnerabilities can be anything from weaknesses in hardware and software through to a weakness in an organizational process, policy or human awareness and behaviour. Vulnerabilities will be explored in depth in Chapter 3 (technical vulnerabilities) and Chapters 5 and 6 (in relation to social engineering).

Cyber security and the law

The importance of cyber security has become more widely accepted in recent years. The topic has become unavoidable, with more people, organizations and governments suffering from cyber attacks or issues of cyber insecurity. This leads to cyber security hitting the headlines more frequently, which in turn raises more awareness. At the same time, organizations are expected to work towards compliance with various pieces of legislation and regulation that concern cyber security. There is no one cyber security law in the UK, but multiple legal requirements are covered in the Computer Misuse Act 1990, Communications Act 2003, Privacy and Electronic Communications Regulations 2003 (PECR), the Data Protection Act 2018 (DPA) and the General Data Protection Regulation 2018 (GDPR). In certain sectors, other regulations apply as well. For example, firms in the UK that provide financial products and services must adhere to the Financial Conduct Authority's (FCA) *Handbook of Rules and Guidance*. Those providing essential services (for example, oil and gas providers) are subject to the Network and Information Systems Regulations 2018 (NIS Regulations).

Data protection and the GDPR

The DPA and GDPR changed the risk landscape for organizations that process personal data in the UK (and, in terms of the GDPR, any organization around the world that processes the personal data of European citizens). The DPA and GDPR sit alongside one another, with the DPA tailoring how the GDPR (which is a European regulation) is interpreted in the UK.

The DPA and GDPR do not tell organizations what to do or how to do it, but rather set out key principles, rights and obligations for processing personal data, as part of a requirement that organizations keep personal data secure. The requirement is intended to protect against unauthorized or unlawful use of the personal data and against loss, destruction and damage of personal data, with more sensitive personal data (for example, data relating to health or sexuality) requiring more robust security measures. EU countries have national bodies responsible for overseeing the protection of personal data in their jurisdiction. In the UK, this is the Information Commissioner's Office (ICO), which is the UK's independent body set up to uphold information rights.

When the GDPR came into effect, one of the biggest changes it ushered in was in relation to enforcement. In the UK, before the GDPR, organizations could face monetary penalties of a maximum £500,000. Under the GDPR, failure to implement appropriate measures to safeguard personal data can result in a monetary penalty of up to €20 million or 4 per cent of annual global turnover, whichever is the greater figure.

At the time of writing, the largest monetary penalty we have seen associated with the GDPR was in July 2021 when the Luxembourg National Commission for Data Protection (CNPD) fined Amazon $877 million for non-compliance with general data processing principles. There is limited information regarding the case due to Luxembourg's secrecy laws. However, it appears that the action came after a complaint in 2018 from French privacy rights group La Quadrature du Net and it reportedly relates to Amazon Europe Core S.à.r.l.'s targeted advertising practices, specifically relating to security and user consent.[5]

Amazon has appealed the decision and the case is due to be heard at a Luxembourg court in January 2024.[6]

Cyber security and personal lives

Sometimes, the fallout from cyber security issues is deeply personal. In August 2015, cyber criminals hacked Ashley Madison, a dating website for people who are married and seeking discreet illicit affairs. A group called the Impact Team claimed responsibility for the hack and followed up on their threats to release a full database of Ashley Madison customers, which was over 30 million accounts across 40 countries. Impact Team had threatened to take this action unless the Ashley Madison site was shut down by its parent company Avid Life Media (ALM), which ALM refused to comply with. The data that was shared online included people's names, addresses, height, weight, credit card information, passwords, security questions and answers, and sexual preferences and desires. A newspaper in Alabama printed the names of everyone in that region who was listed in the database. There were reports of resignations, physical attacks, blackmail and divorces. Most tragically, there were suicides, including a priest in Louisiana.[7]

ALM, and the breach of Ashley Madison, was subject to a joint investigation by the Privacy Commissioner of Canada (where ALM is based) and the Australian Privacy Commissioner. This investigation did not state a conclusion on how the attack was conducted, but did comment on the security measures that ALM had failed to put in place. The investigation found that ALM lacked a framework to determine whether their approach to security was adequate and that some security safeguards were either insufficient or lacking.[8] The US Federal Trade Commission issued a $1.66 million penalty to ALM (who had rebranded to Ruby Corp by the time the penalty was issued), having reduced the penalty from $17.5 million due to Ruby Corp's inability to pay. In 2017, Ruby Corp agreed to pay $11.2 million to settle litigation in the US, brought on behalf of the 37 million users who had their personal data exposed.

If nothing else, Ashley Madison is a case study that highlights issues of cyber security. Users of the site trusted the organization with deeply personal information and perhaps did not consider the risks, threats, potential vulnerabilities and possible mitigations of doing so. More so, ALM/Ruby Corp failed to put adequate security measures in place, despite being entrusted with extremely sensitive data for millions of people around the world. The fallout had a financial cost for ALM/Ruby Corp, and a deeply personal cost for many people using the website.

This chapter has provided an overview of the fundamental importance of cyber security to us on a personal, organizational and societal level. If I have somehow failed to convince you why cyber security is important then the rest of the book – looking at everything from technical to human to nation-state-level cyber issues – should do the job.

Notes

1   YouTube (2019) YouTube for press, www.youtube.com/intl/en-GB/about/press (archived at https://perma.cc/AM8M-5FEM)
2   Facebook Investor Relation (2019) Facebook reports third quarter 2019 results, Facebook, 30 October, https://investor.fb.com/investor-news/press-release-details/2019/Facebook-Reports-Third-Quarter-2019-Results/default.aspx (archived at https://perma.cc/AD5V-QYZ4)
3   Forbes (2019) The world's most valuable brands, www.forbes.com/powerful-brands/list (archived at https://perma.cc/547C-EZ2F)
4   World Economic Forum (2019) The Global Risks Report, www.weforum.org/reports/global-risks-report-2023/in-full/1-global-risks-2023-today-s-crisis (archived at https://perma.cc/64TV-V88S)
5   https://www.corderycompliance.com/amazon-fine-lux-cnpd/ (archived at https://perma.cc/ER68-K3SE)
6   https://www.infosecurity-magazine.com/magazine-features/fines-data-protection-violations/ (archived at https://perma.cc/DVY9-DKP3)

7   Lamont, T (2016) Life after the Ashley Madison affair, *Observer*, 28 February, www.theguardian.com/technology/2016/feb/28/what-happened-after-ashley-madison-was-hacked (archived at https://perma.cc/WBZ2-CKFJ)
8   Office of the Privacy Commissioner of Canada, 2016 PIPEDA Report of Findings 2016-005, 22 August, www.priv.gc.ca/en/opc-actions-and-decisions/investigations/investigations-into-businesses/2016/pipeda-2016-005 (archived at https://perma.cc/LKM6-5FY4)

PART TWO

The technical side of cyber security

CHAPTER THREE

Technical vulnerabilities

Every year, more and more technical vulnerabilities are reported by security researchers. It's important that the security industry keeps up to date with vulnerabilities and their details, so that we can respond appropriately and put mitigations in place – however you use your new cyber security skills in your life and career, you will need to keep abreast of this kind of technical vulnerability. Fortunately, there are tools already around to help you cultivate your vulnerability awareness.

Common Vulnerabilities and Exposures list

The CVE list is a tool run by the National Cybersecurity Federally Funded Research and Development Centre (FFRDC), and operated by the Mitre Corporation. The CVE list is a publicly available database of known information security vulnerabilities and exposures, providing common names and reference points for these vulnerabilities, making it easier to share information about them within the cyber security community.

Common Weakness Enumeration

Common Weakness Enumeration (CWE™) is a list of hardware and software weakness types that have security implications. The list is developed by the community and enables us to use a common language to identify and describe security weaknesses. The CWE list was first released in 2006 and is a resource for security practitioners and developers to search, view and download.[1]

It took a while to get here. How the cyber security community references and tracks vulnerabilities has evolved over the last few decades:

- The US Computer Emergency Response Team (CERT) advisories began publicly listing vulnerabilities in 1988, taking an approach that communicated vulnerabilities along with details on how to check and fix the issues.
- Bugtraq utilized a similar system to the CERT advisories. Operating as a precursor to the CVE system, it was created in 1993 by Scott Chasin as an electronic mailing list. Bugtraq's approach differed from the CERT advisory in that vulnerabilities were released even if the vendor had not responded.
- The original concept for what would become the CVE list was presented by the co-creators of CVE, David E Mann and Steven M Christey, in 1999 at Purdue University in Indiana. From that original concept, a working group was formed and the first CVE list, detailing 321 entries, was publicly launched in September 1999.[2]

The CVE list has grown exponentially over the last 20 years, with CVEs now issued on an almost daily basis. In the year 2000, there were 1,020 CVEs issued, in 2018 there were 16,556, and in 2022 there were 25,227.[3] This shows the huge growth in vulnerabilities being identified and reported, which in turn demonstrates the large workload and increasing complexity that is part of protecting people, systems and organizations from attacks.

Common Vulnerability Scoring System

To help us make sense of CVEs – increasingly important when so many are being issued – there is the Common Vulnerability Scoring System (CVSS). CVSS is an open industry standard, assigning severity scores to vulnerabilities, which enables security professionals and organizations to understand the potential impact and prioritize a plan of action to fix them. Scores for a vulnerability range from 0–10, with 10 being the most severe rating that can be ascribed. The scores are determined by metrics that relate to three facets of any given vulnerability:

- the intrinsic qualities that are constant over time and across user environments (base);
- the qualities that change over time (temporal); and
- the characteristics that vary according to the context of the vulnerability or system (environment).

In order to work in cyber security, you don't necessarily need to understand *all* the intricacies of CVEs and how the CVSS works, but you might want to consider getting familiar with the basics to keep your knowledge up to date. At the time of writing, CVSSv3.01 is the current system in use to score CVEs.

Open Web Application Security Project top ten

With so many technical vulnerabilities in existence, and more being identified and reported all the time, it is overwhelming to think about how we navigate these without a good system in place. This is where the Open Web Application Security Project (OWASP) top ten comes in. OWASP is a vendor-neutral, worldwide not-for-profit charitable organization that focuses on improving the security of software by enabling people and organizations to make informed security decisions.

Periodically, OWASP publishes a list of the top ten most critical web application security risks, which is compiled from project members, security experts and industry contributors.[4] This means that the cyber security community can know where and how to focus their most urgent action and attention – it's really a vital tool in what can be an overwhelming slew of information!

The OWASP web application top ten, as published in 2021 is:

1 Broken Access Control
2 Cryptographic Failures
3 Injection
4 Insecure Design
5 Security Misconfiguration
6 Vulnerable and Outdated Components
7 Identification and Authentication Failures
8 Software and Data Integrity Failures
9 Security Logging and Monitoring Failures
10 Server-Side Request Forgery

Let's go through each of these, so that we have a basic understanding of the most threatening technical vulnerabilities around today.

1. Broken access control

In 2021, broken access control moved into the top spot, having been ranked fifth in the OWASP top ten in 2017. Access controls are in place to prevent someone from gaining access beyond their permissions. Therefore, broken access control is the circumvention of security mechanisms or the wrong use of access control; for example, bypassing the controls guarding a website by modifying the URL to gain admin actions without having admin access. To use an example from the physical world to bring this to life, broken access control would be if we gained access to a locked room because the padlock was only attached to the doorframe, and we could simply open the door.

2. Cryptographic failures

Previously labelled 'sensitive data exposure', this category has been re-scoped (as well as renamed) to address the root cause of these issues: cryptographic failures refers to a lack of cryptography which results in sensitive data exposure. Systems today hold many pieces of data. Since the 1990s and the explosion of the World Wide Web, organizations put more and more information online, including personal and sensitive information. This category, therefore, relates to the failure to use up-to-date and adequate cryptography to sufficiently protect data.

3. Injection

Rated number 1 in the 2017 top ten, injection flaws allow an attacker to 'inject' data into a system, which can then enable the attacker to execute commands or access data without proper authorization. One of the most devastating injection attack vectors is against applications that use a structured query language (SQL) database for their backend data management.

SQL is the standard language for database management, and SQL injection has been used in many cyber attacks.

CASE STUDY   LearnPress Plugin

WordPress often – rather unfairly – gets a bad press when it comes to security. The security issues with WordPress are generally not connected to the main platform itself, but to plugins. In November and December 2022, the WordPress security company Patchstack found that 100,000 WordPress sites were vulnerable to multiple critical flaws introduced by the plugin LearnPress, a Learning Management System (LMS) that enables website developers to create and sell online courses on their websites without needing to code themselves.

Patchstack discovered the following vulnerabilities in LearnPress:

- CVE-2022-47615: an unauthenticated local file inclusion (LFI) flaw that could expose credentials, authorization tokens, and API keys, facilitating further compromise.

- CVE-2022-45808: an unauthenticated SQL injection that could lead to sensitive information disclosure, data modification, and arbitrary code execution.

- CVE-2022-45820: an unauthenticated SQL injection flaw in two shortcodes of the plugin.

Patchstack followed a vulnerability disclosure process and informed the vendor of their findings, and the vendor responded by quickly fixing the issues and publishing a patch.[5]

---

4. Insecure design

Insecure design was a new category in the 2021 OWASP top ten, and broadly relates to 'missing or ineffective control design'.[6] By including this category of flaw, OWASP are attempting to influence the community to focus on pre-coding activities that are crucial to a 'secure by design' approach. These pre-coding activities relate to the development of a culture and methodology that evaluates threats and supports secure coding practices, with the integration of threat modelling and the pursuit of a secure development lifecycle.

5. Security misconfiguration

Perhaps the largest category on the OWASP list is the security misconfiguration section. Almost all server-side issues are due to misconfiguration; these can vary from default accounts being left unchanged through to unprotected files and directories. There are many issues that fall into this category, and with the rise of Internet of Things (IoT) devices that often have weak or default passwords (as we see in the analysis of the Dyn DDoS on page 82) the relevance of this category is only likely to keep increasing.

6. Vulnerable and outdated components

This category relates to components of a system that are no longer being supported by the developer, where you do not know all the components you are using or where you do not know whether your components are vulnerable. This category also applies to environments where patches are applied on a schedule (for example, monthly) and so there is a period of time where the technology (and therefore, the organization) is exposed.

7. Identification and authentication failures

Previously labelled Broken Authentication (which was second in the 2017 top ten), this category has been broadened to include identification failures. Identification and authentication failures refers to a lack of confirmation of a user's identity, authentication, and session management. Such weaknesses can include credential stuffing (for example by enabling an attacker to run automated scripts of usernames and passwords to attempt to access accounts on a website), brute force attacks, permitting weak passwords and not implementing two-factor authentication.

8. Software and data integrity failures

This is a new category for 2021 and relates to code and infra-structure that does not protect against integrity violations. For example, if an application relies on an insecure plug-in, as we see in the LearnPress case study. This category highlights the inter-dependency of software and the way in which vulnerabilities can emerge from our reliance on other sources.

CASE STUDY SolarWinds

The SolarWinds Orion attack highlights the vulnerabilities that can emerge from the interdependency of software more acutely than any incident we have seen before. Microsoft President Brad Smith described it as 'the largest and most sophisticated sort of operation that we have seen' in a US Senate select committee.[7]

In December 2020, the US cybersecurity firm FireEye discovered that an update in the SolarWinds Orion platform was compromised, enabling the attacker to send administrator-level commands to any affected installation. The update had been released in March of that year and, as it is good security practice to install updates, it was downloaded by 18,000 clients. Analysis from SolarWinds concluded that while 18,000 customers downloaded the update, the attack ultimately affected 'only' approximately 100 companies and nine US federal agencies, including Microsoft, Cisco, Deloitte, the Department of Homeland Security and the Department of the Treasury.

The UK and US security agencies announced, following investigation, that Russia's Foreign Intelligence Service (SVR) was behind this attack, with the UK National Cyber Security Centre describing it as 'one of the most serious cyber intrusions of recent times'.[8]

---

9. Security logging and monitoring failures

Monitoring and logging events that happen on your systems is key – not only for discovery and remediation of technical issues, but also for allowing accurate forensic reconstruction of cybercrime, which is important for investigation and attribution. Attributing the actions of people using and attacking systems is key to convictions; exploiting a lack of logging is a gift to attackers who seek to cover their tracks. However, in practice, logging is not as straightforward as it may seem. Organizations often have sufficient logs in place but are unable to sort or filter the logging sufficiently to find attacks. It can be overwhelming for analysts who can be inundated with alerts and false positives, making it hard to see the real issues. The appropriate level of logging and monitoring is a delicate balancing act that needs constant feedback and removal of systems if they do not provide adequate value.

10. Server-side request forgery

This new category was added to the top ten by OWASP as it came from their community survey (along with Vulnerable and Outdated Components), and so it is a category which Application Security Researchers in the OWASP community are concerned about. Server-Side Request Forgery (SSRF) exploits the trust relationship between the application and the server, allowing the attacker to use the server against itself. For example, if an application has the ability to retrieve an image on your server, such as your profile image, an attacker could potentially exploit SSRF to retrieve a different file from the server which they would not ordinarily be authorized to see.

CASE STUDY   WannaCry

In May 2017, an unprecedented cyber attack hit the world. The WannaCrypt (WannaCry) ransomware attack began on Friday 12 May and spread globally within one day, targeting computers running Microsoft Windows 7 that were vulnerable to an exploit called EternalBlue.

Microsoft had released a patch to fix the exploit, but one month after the patch was released, WannaCry had still spread to 300,000 computers across at least 150 countries.[9] These computers had either not applied the patch, or were using 'end-of-life' Windows systems (meaning that they were deemed past the point of useful life by Microsoft and so not supported in the patch). The UK National Health Service (NHS) was particularly affected, with one-third of hospital trusts and 8 per cent of GP practices hit; in total, 19,000 appointments had to be cancelled and the attack cost the NHS £20 million between 12–19 May and a further £72 million in clean-up and upgrade costs.[10] The NHS, and other organizations that were victims of WannaCry, were criticized by many for failing to install the patch. Whilst this criticism is understandable, it is also short-sighted: patching may seem simple, but in practice it can be very complicated. As the NHS has acknowledged, patching is not simple when you are managing a large estate with tens of thousands of machines, especially when patching a device could disrupt patient care.[11]

WannaCry is a ransomware cryptoworm that encrypts data and demands payment in bitcoin in exchange for the decrypt key. It automatically self-propagates, scanning vulnerable systems and then gaining access via EternalBlue and using a tool called DoublePulsar to install and execute a copy of itself. The attack was halted when the security researcher MalwareTech analysed a piece of code from the malware and noticed an unregistered domain, which he then registered. He knew from experience that this would be a good thing to do, but what he didn't realize was that this would actually be the 'kill switch' that stopped the attack.[12]

WannaCry makes a fascinating and worrying case study for many reasons. Not least, it highlights our global dependency on connected technology for services as life-or-death important as healthcare. It also has interesting geo-political dimensions, which we will return to in Chapter 10.

CASE STUDY   Log4Shell

In December 2021, a vulnerability was disclosed which caused big waves in the global security community and halted holiday celebrations for many security teams. As an isolated example, one federal cabinet department in the USA dedicated 33,000 hours to responding to the Log4Shell vulnerability, which inevitably impacted other mission-critical work[13]. Jen Easterly, Director of the US Cybersecurity and Infrastructure Agency (CISA), described the vulnerability as 'one of the most serious I've seen in my entire career, if not the most serious'[14]

Apache Log4j is a library of code that is widely used in many websites. To understand some Log4Shell, first we need to understand Log4j. Here's how we described Log4j to readers of our website (the cup of coffee analogy is hard to beat, so bears repeating for you here):

When you write some code, you often don't write everything, this is inefficient as you would have to keep rewriting the same bits of code for similar tasks. People, and large companies, share their code for doing specific things to help others. This can be strange to understand for some non-technical people but here is a good analogy to explain it.

Imagine you have the task of making coffee for your partner every morning. A simple task on the face of it but breaking it down you need more and more components. You need a cup, you need water (hot water), you need coffee, and you may need milk and sugar.

You don't go to the pottery and make a new cup every morning, nor do you milk a cow or pick and dry coffee beans and then grind them up. You certainly don't pump water up from a well, filter it, heat it, and then combine everything. That would be incredibly time- and labour-intensive. Instead – if you're like most people at least – you buy a ready-made cup, buy pre-packaged coffee, milk and sugar. You turn on the tap for pre-filtered water, then you combine them in a manner that suits your needs.

The milk, water, cup and coffee are all essentially libraries, you can 'import' the milk into any other recipe you are building that day: a bowl of cereal, a cake, scrambled eggs, more coffee etc. That is the power of a library and of code in general – write once, use many times!

When you build an application, you need a way to record every thing that happens within it. This is where a log comes in, as it is basically like a huge diary of everything that happens to an application: which end-user did what, when, how, where from, etc. The general rule of thumb is the more logging you have the easier it is to find and fix problems for your end-users, and you can also keep an eye on anything suspicious going on. The Log4j project run by Apache Foundation is considered one of the easiest and most robust libraries for performing logging.[15]

In November 2021, the cloud security team at Alibaba discovered a vulnerability in Log4j which became known as Log4Shell. The vulnerability allows the code to download and execute whatever the attacker tells to. This includes backdoors and so essentially, Log4Shell gives an attacker the potential to perform Remote Code Execution – AKA giving them the power to do whatever they want to do with your machine. Remote Code Execution (or RCE) is very bad news. The Log4Shell vulnerability had existed unnoticed in the code since 2013 and, once reported, was given a severity rating of 10, the highest available. It was estimated to affect hundreds of millions of devices worldwide and many security experts agree that it is the worst security vulnerability we have ever seen.

Log4j is deeply embedded in many systems around the world and so the impact of Log4Shell is likely to be felt for some time. In November 2022, one year after Log4Shell was discovered by Alibaba, Tenable reported that they had found that 72 per cent of organizations remain vulnerable to the Log4Shell vulnerability. This analysis was based on data collected from over 500 million tests up to October 2022.[16] The United States Cyber Safety Review Board reported that 'Log4j is an "endemic vulnerability" and that vulnerable instances of Log4j will remain in systems for many years to come, perhaps a decade or longer'.[17]

What technology is vulnerable?

When the OWASP top ten was first created, smart phones had not come of age. Times have changed since then, and now it is estimated that 5 billion people have mobile phones and half of these are smart phones.[18] When large numbers of people embrace a form of digital technology, it is unfortunately inevitable that cyber criminals will be seeking to exploit that technology for their own gain. It is also inevitable that these devices will be vulnerable to technical flaws in much the same way that computers are. Whilst this chapter has looked at web applications, the vulnerabilities covered relate to mobile applications too: they are vulnerabilities that exist in code and connected technology, and are not specific to platforms.

Beyond this, it is important to understand that many industrial systems are vulnerable to the same technical weaknesses that this chapter covers. Supervisory control and data acquisition (SCADA) networks comprise hardware and applications that control and monitor vital industrial control systems (ICS) for key infrastructure around the world, including gas, electricity, nuclear power and water. SCADA systems are efficient, enable quick communication of issues and provide real-time data that can be very helpful and valuable. Unfortunately, many SCADA networks are also vulnerable to security flaws. A study of 850 ICS and SCADA networks, across six continents and all industrial sectors, found that 69 per cent used plain-text passwords, 40 per cent had direct connections to the internet and 57 per cent had weak anti-virus protection.[19]

Software and hardware devices that are connected to the internet bring us much in the way of benefits, at a personal, organizational and societal level. At the same time, the more connected we become, the more we open ourselves up to vulnerabilities, many of which we have been aware of for decades and seem, on the face of it, very simple. We must continue to strive for a better foundation of security in the systems, software and products that we use. This requires a layered defence, not relying on one technical solution as the only line of defence but using many. Anti-virus, firewalls, patching, careful configuration of systems, actionable monitoring and logging, appropriate authentication and suitable encryption are all part of these foundations.

I am not calling them basic measures, because that would imply they are easy; but they are foundations because cyber security relies on us to get them right and to layer up these solutions so that, in the event one or more are breached, others may withstand attack. Finally, if the defences fail and an attack is realized, a segmented network can help damage limitation. WannaCry is a stark example of what can happen when networks are 'flat', with no barriers in place to stop attacks from moving laterally. With technical vulnerabilities, and cyber security in general, we cannot simply work to defend ourselves; we must also recognize that attacks happen and plan an active approach to defence, asking how we can contain attacks and what we should do in the face of a breach.

In the next chapter, we will explore some of these themes in more detail, by addressing why people are so central to cyber security. The technology lifecycle that can be affected by so many vulnerabilities, some of which we have covered in this chapter, requires human interaction at every stage – the way in which people interact with technology can have a huge impact on cyber security.

Notes

1 https://cwe.mitre.org/about/ (archived at https://perma.cc/9AHM-XHXY)
2 Mitre Corporation (2018) History, 10 December, https://cve.mitre.org/about/ history.html (archived at https://perma.cc/SUD7-D4EA)
3 Özkan, S (2010) CVE details, www.cvedetails.com (archived at https://perma. cc/WQ9C-X3WM)
4 A web application is any computer program that uses web browsers and technology to function over the internet, for example ecommerce websites, email services, social media websites and online forms.
5 https://patchstack.com/articles/multiple-critical-vulnerabilities-fixed-in-learnpress-plugin-version/ (archived at https://perma.cc/KR2U-JWLN)
6 https://owasp.org/Top10/A04_2021-Insecure_Design/ (archived at https:// perma.cc/N8DX-ZFAL)

7 https://www.theguardian.com/technology/2021/feb/23/solarwinds-hack-senate-hearing-microsoft (archived at https://perma.cc/AVC7-XC8V)
8 https://www.ncsc.gov.uk/collection/ncsc-annual-review-2021/the-threat/solarwinds (archived at https://perma.cc/TR28-SUTJ)
9 European Union Agency for Law Enforcement Cooperation (Europol) (2017) Internet organized crime threat assessment 2017, www.europol.europa.eu (archived at https://perma.cc/8CGG-NGYE)
10 Department of Health and Social Care (2018) Securing cyber resilience in health and care: Progress update, October, https://assets.publishing.service.gov.uk/government/uploads/system/uploads/attachment_data/file/747464/securing-cyber-resilience-in-health-and-care-september-2018-update.pdf (archived at https://perma.cc/62X2-42JP)
11 House of Commons Committee of Public Accounts (2018) Cyber-attack on the NHS: Thirty-second report of session 2017–19, https://publications.parliament.uk/pa/cm201719/cmselect/cmpubacc/787/787.pdf (archived at https://perma.cc/QJ9D-4JNC)
12 MalwareTech (2017) How to accidentally stop a global cyber attacks (blog), MalwareTech: Life of a malware analyst, 13 May, www.malwaretech.com/2017/05/how-to-accidentally-stop-a-global-cyber-attacks.html (archived at https://perma.cc/NK4N-TEKD)
13 https://www.cisa.gov/sites/default/files/publications/CSRB-Report-on-Log4-July-11-2022_508.pdf (archived at https://perma.cc/774V-SUZY)
14 https://www.ft.com/content/d3c244f2-eaba-4c46-9a51-b28fc13d9551 (archived at https://perma.cc/XJ4G-UWWM)
15 https://www.cygenta.co.uk/post/log4shell-in-simple-terms (archived at https://perma.cc/88C4-LV56)
16 https://www.tenable.com/press-releases/tenable-research-finds-72-of-organizations-remain-vulnerable-to-nightmare-log4j (archived at https://perma.cc/RL6R-EGJR)
17 https://www.cisa.gov/sites/default/files/publications/CSRB-Report-on-Log4-July-11-2022_508.pdf (archived at https://perma.cc/BB9B-9XEP)
18 Silver, L (2019) Smartphone ownership is growing rapidly around the world, but not always equally (blog), Pew Research Center, 5 February, www.pewresearch.org/global/2019/02/05/smartphone-ownership-is-growing-rapidly-around-the-world-but-not-always-equally (archived at https://perma.cc/MAE5-2ATA)
19 CyberX (2019) Global ICS and IIoT risk report, https://cyberx-labs.com/resources/risk-report-2019/#download-form (archived at https://perma.cc/Y26N-XTXD)

PART THREE

The human side of cyber security

CHAPTER FOUR

Why people are so important in cyber security

People are at the heart of cyber security. We're not protecting technology for the sake of the technology, or even protecting information for the sake of the information. We are doing it, ultimately, to protect people. To protect their finances, their jobs, their identities and sometimes even their physical safety. There are a number of different ways in which people represent the foundation of cyber security; we can look at different stages of the technology lifecycle to understand how people are central to the protection of technology and its interaction with information. In this chapter, we'll cover the technology lifecycle:

- design;
- creation;
- testing;
- use;
- abuse;
- destruction.

Design

The way hardware, software, technology and information systems are designed is central to the security of those systems, which of course relies upon the people involved with the design. In cyber security, many problems are rooted in flawed design; if security is built into technology, then it would be tackled at the root cause.

The UK National Cyber Security Centre (NCSC) advocate an approach they call 'Secure by Default':

> To be truly effective, security needs to be built-in from the ground up. Hardware needs to be designed to resist physical attacks, and provide secure storage to other components. Operating systems need to take advantage of hardware security features, and applications need to use the right operating system security features.[1]

A Secure by Default approach involves individuals, teams and organizations building security in at the start of a project, which relies upon an acknowledgement of the importance of security as a first principle. Entrepreneurs and organizations understandably often want to move fast: they want to design, build and release technology as soon as possible, to gain market advantage and increase profits. However, the problem with moving fast is that it can lead to security being overlooked at the start of a project, and instead becoming an afterthought.

Secure by Default encourages an approach that makes security a foundational principle but without hampering usability, enabling people to use the product in a secure way without having to configure certain features or follow behaviours that are not intuitive. It is an approach that recognizes that security is fundamental to good design, but should not be something that is difficult for the end user to engage with.

Creation

Building secure products and services involves ensuring that the process of making those products and services has security at its heart. This builds upon the Secure by Default approach we have just covered, requiring that the manufacturing process considers security at every stage. Those who are responsible for creating technology must assess the process from every angle with security in mind, and this involves mitigating the potential for accidental and malicious insider threats.

In modern production, it is common for different elements in the manufacturing process to be created at different places by different suppliers. This means it can be much more difficult for producers to have complete oversight of every stage of production, which potentially increases the potential for accidents and/ or malicious insiders to introduce gaps or flaws in security.

Testing

The testing stage is crucial for security. This relies upon people in many regards: the creator or developer recognizing the need for good testing, and allowing for the time it takes as well as understanding what 'good testing' involves; the skills and objectivity of the testers; and the willingness and ability of the creator or developer to take any results from the testing and incorporate any changes needed.

Security testing can take many forms, depending upon what needs to be assessed. A piece of code, a new door and a process for organizing paperwork are all things which may need assessing from a security perspective – but how you would do so varies. A piece of code would be analysed by a penetration tester to identify whether it contained any bugs or malicious code. A penetration tester with expertise in physical security could assess

THE HUMAN SIDE OF CYBER SECURITY

a new door to identify whether there are any flaws in how it was installed or whether security controls on the door are lacking or could be circumvented. A process for organizing paperwork would assess what paperwork is being handled and by whom, where it will be transported and stored, how this process will be logged, and who could have access to it at any point. The extent to which all of this testing and assessing is completed to a standard that benefits security depends on the skills and mindset of the testers as well as the willingness and ability of the creator to take feedback.

A very human part of a security tester's job is to understand both the legal and ethical elements of what they do and have a careful consideration of both. For example, a penetration tester can be exposed to a great deal of personal and organizational data throughout the course of their work. They may discover information about an individual or company's activities that they find morally ambiguous, but not illegal. Adhering to professional ethics is a fundamental part of being a security tester (we will explore ethics in more detail later in this chapter).

Use

How we interact with technology and information has many security implications, which is why cyber security awareness-raising training is so important in organizations. When people think of the insider threat in cyber security, they often think immediately of the malicious insider threat. However, the non-malicious insider threat – the accidental insider – is much more common. The accidental insider is someone just trying to do their job, but because of how a system is designed or built – or how they use a system or interact with information – they make a mistake that causes a breach. It could be a weak password, which is compromised by a cyber criminal, or talking about company confidential information on a crowded train. It could be clicking a malicious link in a phishing email, accidentally emailing a sensitive file to the wrong person or making errors in how a system is set up, thereby exposing more data than intended.

CASE STUDY   Amazon S3

Amazon Simple Storage Service (S3) buckets are cloud-based storage systems that can store huge amounts of data (think Dropbox on a massive scale). Amazon S3 stores data for millions of applications for companies around the world. It's popular because it is seen as a cost-effective and scalable solution for storing huge amounts of data, but research from Symantec found that more than 70 million records were stolen or leaked in 2018 as a result of poorly configured Amazon S3 buckets.[2]

Some breaches that were the result of misconfigured Amazon S3 buckets include:

- In September 2021, the research team at vpnMentor reported their discovery that the personal data of 700,000 students in Ghana was openly available on the internet, unencrypted and largely not password protected – in an open Amazon S3 bucket. This information had apparently been exposed on the internet from 2018 onwards and included personal information, scans of ID cards and employment records. This potentially exposed hundreds of thousands of people in Ghana to identity theft, fraud and phishing. Furthermore, it could have provided attackers with a means to impersonate legitimate employees of an organization and gain access to that organization's information or systems.[3]

- In July 2022, 3 terabytes of data relating to airport employees in Peru and Colombia was reportedly found in an open Amazon S3 bucket. This included airport employee records, ID card photos, and personally identifiable information (PII) that included names, photos, occupations, and national ID numbers. Again, this potentially exposed the individuals to identity theft, fraud and phishing. It poses a wider threat to national security and the aviation industry, especially as the data also included information on planes, fuel lines and GPS coordinates.[4]

• In December 2022, an open Amazon S3 bucket was discovered online exposing the information of over 100,000 students. The bucket, belonging to the publishing giant McGraw-Hill, contained over 22 terabytes of information and had apparently been openly available online since 2015. The 117 million files contained students' names and email addresses for US and Canadian students as well as leaking the private digital keys of McGraw-Hill, which could have enabled access to the company's sensitive data and source code.[5]

How we use technology at home also has significant implications for cyber security. From a personal perspective, the way we engage with technology can have an impact on security for ourselves, our families and society at large. Unfortunately, a lot of technology – and the internet in general – has not been designed according to the Secure by Default principle. This means that it is often unclear to the average person how to engage with good cyber security practices at home. Products often don't come with security built in or security features turned on by default, meaning that the burden for security often falls to the end-user. This is not realistic: in my opinion, it is not fair to ask people to add security to the technology they buy or engage with, not least because there is a reasonable expectation that this will have already been accounted for by the manufacturer. We do not ask people to go through extra steps to make sure the soft furnishings they buy are fire resistant or the car they rent has been safety-tested, but we apparently do expect them to be security experts when it comes to digital technology.

When people engage with digital technology, they are doing so because they want to interact with the benefits of the technology. They want to use their email or social media account to communicate with people. They want to use a smart watch to track their fitness. They want to set up home CCTV cameras to check on their house when it is empty or check on their baby while they are in another room.

While it may be unreasonable and unfair to expect people to configure all of the digital technology that they use from a security point of view, that is the situation that we're in. How individuals manage passwords, share information, and set up and use their digital devices can play a huge part in cyber security at many levels.

None of this, to be clear, is intended to victim-blame. It is my strong belief that digital technology should be designed, built and tested in such a way that people can use it securely and intuitively, protected against those who seek to identify and abuse security weaknesses for their own gain. However, the reality is that how we use technology can have a profound effect on cyber security.

The personal level

There are, unfortunately, many ways in which cybercrime can affect individuals, and how we engage with digital technology plays a part in the extent to which we are protected from cybercrime. For example, the passwords I use, and whether I re-use those passwords or have unique ones for each of my accounts, impacts the level of security that is applied to those online accounts. If I use weak passwords, I risk those passwords being guessed (either by an individual or one of millions of common passwords being checked by a computer script) and my accounts being illegally accessed by others. If I use the same password for multiple accounts and one of those accounts is breached, I run the risk of my other accounts being accessed (like dominoes, when one account falls, others may be knocked over too). This is what happened with the PayPal 'hack' (that really wasn't a hack) in 2022.

In December 2022, PayPal discovered that criminals had used credential stuffing to gain access to nearly 35,000 accounts on their platform. This means they had access to the personal and financial details stored in those accounts. As soon as PayPal realized, they reset the passwords of those compromised accounts and so kicked the criminals out, apparently within two days of the compromise.

It appears that that accounts were compromised via 'credential stuffing', in which criminals access people's accounts by using login details that the individual has used elsewhere and that have been previously stolen. There have been many cases of websites being breached and account holders' usernames and passwords being stolen. These details often end up being shared or sold on the dark web; many cyber criminals can then use the details to attempt to log in to hundreds of thousands of other websites using automated technology. This is the big problem with an individual re-using passwords: if that password is compromised once, it can potentially enable access to any other account where you are re-using it. This also shows the importance of two-factor or multi-factor authentication, which adds a double layer of security to online accounts and so passwords are not the only line of defence between your data and cyber criminals.

TWO-FACTOR AUTHENTICATION

Two-factor authentication (2FA) acts like a second layer of defence on your online accounts, and most websites where you make an account (email, social media, popular shopping sites) have 2FA available. You set 2FA up in the security settings of your accounts and, at its most basic level, it involves entering your mobile phone number. Then, when you try to access the account from a device that you don't usually use, the website requires you to enter, as well as your password, a unique one-time code that is sent to your mobile by SMS. This means that if your password is compromised in any way, and a criminal attempts to get into your account with it, they would need the unique code that is sent to you by SMS message. The benefit of this is twofold: your account is better protected, and if you receive a 2FA code without prompting the site for one, it's a very strong indicator that your password has been compromised and you should change it (on that site and, if you are re-using that password, anywhere else).

SIM SWAP ATTACKS

2FA is good. It adds a much higher level of security to accounts compared to using passwords alone, especially if those passwords are weak and being used for more than one account. However, like everything in cyber security, it is not perfect. We do what we can to mitigate risks and balance usability and security.

The vulnerability with SMS2FA comes from SIM swap attacks. Mobile phone providers are set up in such a way that if you lose your phone, have it stolen or want to change providers, you can keep the same telephone number and change SIM. Criminals take advantage of this in a SIM swap attack. They use personal information on the target, often gathered through social engineering attacks such as phishing emails or bought from other criminals on the dark web, and pose as the target to communicate with the mobile phone provider, convincing the provider to move the target's telephone number to a new SIM, one in their possession. When this happens, the target loses network connection on their phone (their mobile is cut off because their number is no longer attached to their SIM) and instead the criminal receives all calls and SMS text messages going to the target's number. Therefore, the criminal receives any one-time 2FA codes that are sent to that number and, if they already have your password, they are able to bypass the two security factors that comprise 2FA.

For some, SIM swap attacks were understood to be very targeted; a criminal has to single you out to go to the effort of posing as you with the mobile phone provider and accessing your call and SMS text communications. It seemed like the kind of attack that was not too likely to affect the average person, and more likely to be targeted at high-profile and wealthy individuals. However, in early 2019 the City of London Police's Action Fraud team reported a 20-fold increase in SIM swap attacks from 2015 to 2018.[6] With the ease by which SIM cards can be bought in bulk, online for example, and the potential for lucrative return on investment, enabling criminals to clear out people's life savings or their cryptocurrency and apply for loans using the target's details, it should not surprise us that SIM swap attacks have increased and will continue to increase. To protect ourselves, we can set up provisions with the mobile phone provider to keep the SIM locked unless they are provided with a passcode, password or in-person request combined with identification (depending on the provider). Having strong, unique passwords and being wary of social engineering attempts also helps ward off SIM swap attacks. Noticing if our phone goes out of service and contacting the provider as soon as possible will help identify, and possibly halt, a SIM swap attack if it is taking place. Finally, using a more sophisticated form of 2FA, not simply SMS based, adds a higher level of defence to our accounts.

For a more sophisticated form of 2FA, we can look to authentication apps and tokens. Authentication apps are not vulnerable to SIM swap attacks. Instead of sending you a one-time code, most authentication apps such as Google Authenticator will generate random six-digit codes that stay synced with your online services. Another option, arguably more secure again, is to add a layer of hardware protection on to your accounts via a Universal 2nd Factor (U2F) token such as YubiKey. U2F tokens are small USB devices that you plug into your computer (some also work with phones) and use to authenticate yourself in combination with your passwords.

2FA FATIGUE

The more we add layers of defence to our security, the more criminals will seek to evade those layers. To evade 2FA, some attacks will use what is known as 2FA bombing, exploiting 2FA fatigue. The Uber breach of September 2022 highlights how this plays out, as described by the attacker themselves.

According to the person behind the Uber breach, they had the credentials of an employee at Uber. However, they could not access the Uber account with the username and password alone; the employee had 2FA enabled. They circumvented this with a social engineering attack on the target employee, 'spamming' them with multiple 2FA requests over an hour to grind their defences down. When the employee didn't respond, the attacker allegedly sent them a WhatsApp message masquerading as Uber IT and instructing them to accept the 2FA request. The criminal behind this attack then claimed they were able to access Uber databases and source code. They also seemingly accessed Uber's bug bounty vulnerability reports, which of course poses an even greater threat to the company as they are likely to contain sensitive information about vulnerabilities which could be used (or sold) to compromise them again in future.

It's frustrating that so much of the security burden falls to end-users of digital technology, but that's the situation we're in. As criminals continue to find ways to circumvent security controls, we must continue to raise awareness of enhanced controls and how people can engage with them to better protect themselves.

The work level

The first step in social engineering attacks is reconnaissance. Criminals use information available online to gather details of an individual, building a picture of their life in a way that enables them to pose as that individual or to pose as someone that individual would trust. For example, a cyber criminal may be targeting a large corporation for their intellectual property. Using information found in press releases and media articles, they identify law firms that represent the corporation. Turning to the websites of the law firms and social media, particularly professional networking sites such as LinkedIn, they identify which firms represent work relating to intellectual property for the corporation, and narrow in on the partners that handle those accounts. They map the organizational structure, and the close circle around the partners, including their personal assistants (PAs). The criminals turn to other social media sites, like Facebook, Twitter, Instagram and Snapchat, to build rounded pictures of the lives of their targets in the law firm: the IP partners and their PAs. They accumulate information on where the PAs went to school and university; what their hobbies are; who are their favourite musicians. Where they like to hang out and drink coffee. The nurseries, schools, colleges and universities their children attend. Having identified the structure of the email addresses for the firm (for example, firstname.lastname@lawfirmname.com), the criminals now have many options for crafting a spear-phishing email. They could send a malicious attachment masquerading as a coffee shop voucher or the CV of an old university contact looking for a new job. They could send an email that appears to come from their child's school, prompting a reply which – coming from a professional email account – would no doubt include an email signature with their target's mobile phone number included. They could then pose as a client or colleague in a spoofed WhatsApp message to the number they have managed to acquire. Unfortunately, the list is long. This is not to say that people should not use social media or should be paranoid about the information that is publicly available about them, but it is important to understand how information we share can be abused, at a personal and professional level. It goes a long way to be conscious of the information we share, vigilant with the configuration of our privacy settings and wary of unexpected communications encouraging us to share information, transfer money or click links and open documents.

The social level

The Mirai botnet and subsequent Dyn DDoS highlight the extent to which criminals can take advantage of cyber security issues in the home to cause disruption at the society level. Let's take a look at what actually happened and how.

Firstly, we need to define a few concepts:

- A *botnet*: A network of internet-enabled computers (bots) that are all connected and under the control of one centralized computer.
- *DNS*: Standing for Domain Name System, DNS is the way by which the url we type into our web browser (for example, www.confidentcybersecurity.co.uk) is converted into the IP address where the actual website is located (eg 216.58.206.100). DNS is one element of the internet that is incredibly user-friendly: people don't have to know or remember the IP address of the website they want to visit, just the more memorable and descriptive web address, and when they put the web address in the browser, DNS connects the web address to the actual IP address where the website is located. If you're familiar with the old telephone switch system, whereby a caller would speak to a switch operator who would connect who the caller wanted to speak to with the correct number, DNS plays the same role as the switch operator. Without DNS, when we type a web address into our browser, we don't get connected to the IP address we are actually looking for. It is a core part of the internet infrastructure.
- *DoS* and *DDoS*: A Denial of Service (DoS) is when one computer is used, with one internet connection, to flood a targeted website or system with so much traffic that it cannot cope and will no longer function. A Distributed Denial of

Service (DDoS) is when multiple computers and internet connections are used to the same effect. These incidents are not always malicious, they can simply be the result of a website or service coming under more demand than it is built to withstand, but DoS and DDoS are often used to maliciously target organizations or services.

MIRAI AND DYN DDOS

Now let's explore what happened when Dyn (a well-known DNS provider) was hit with a large DDoS. In October 2016, much of the internet was unavailable for large parts of the United States and some of Europe; at the time, many speculated that this was the work of nation-state activity. In the end, it was discovered that the Mirai botnet was the work of three friends in their early twenties, living in the United States, who were looking to gain an advantage in Minecraft.[7] The cause of the outage was the Mirai botnet, which differed from botnets that we had seen until that point because it was composed of Internet of Things (IoT) devices rather than simply computers. In a blog-post at the time, Dyn estimated that the botnet used a network of 100,000 malicious endpoints.[8] Those malicious endpoints were IoT devices, including digital video recorders (DVRs), home routers and home security cameras, which were able to be compromised and used in the botnet because they were protected with only their default (weak) credentials; their owners had not updated the default passwords. Mirai was scripted to scan large sections of the internet, find open Telnet ports and attempt to log in to those devices using 61 username and password combinations that were publicly known to be frequently used as default credentials in such devices.[9] Once logged in, the devices could be used as part of the botnet.

Mirai, and the impact it had on Dyn, makes an interesting case study for a number of reasons. It was an attack that impacted one element of the internet backbone: disrupting DNS disrupts the functioning of the internet. This attack did not just take one website offline; it took thousands offline, which made it a larger DDoS than any which had preceded it. This case was also the first time that IoT devices had been used in a large-scale attack, something which many security experts agree is likely to occur far more frequently in the future, as we connect more IoT devices. The Mirai botnet highlights the fact that cyber attacks can have unintended consequences.

Speculating on attribution and motivation of attacks, without evidence, can be futile: what many assumed to be the work of nation-state attackers attempting to cause large-scale disruption to certain geographies ended up being the work of three young men in their early twenties, citizens of the country that was most impacted, who were simply seeking an advantage in their gaming activities. Collateral damage in cyber attacks is a big problem. People can sometimes believe that a cyber attack would never happen to them or to their organization, because they don't believe that they would be a target of cybercrime. This perspective usually overlooks elements that would make them an attractive target – but not only that, it also discounts the extent to which cybercrime is often not targeted, and the organizations that can be caught up as collateral damage. Finally, this case shows the impact that personal use of technology can have on cyber security at a large scale; and even more so, the inherent weaknesses that can be exposed when digital technology is not built with Secure by Default principles leading the way.

The interdependency between how people use technology and issues of cyber security is why the Secure by Default approach stresses the need for technology to be developed while making security an integral part of products, and also to make it intuitive for the end-user. Blaming end-users for engaging with technology in a way that exposes their information or allows vulnerabilities is simplistic: we need to make security an integral part of technology rather than an add-on which complicates the user experience and opens up weaknesses that criminals can abuse.

Abuse

A fundamental, inescapable element of cyber security is the abuse of technology, systems and information. When it comes to cyber attacks and breaches, people are often keen to attribute blame. If a company gets hacked and valuable data gets into the hands of criminals, there will generally be speculation on what the company did wrong, or did not do right. Of course, it is important for organizations to be responsible when it comes to cyber security, and have measures in place to protect their data (which can be anything from intellectual property to sensitive information on their employees to important data on their customers). However, if we consider a hierarchy of blame, we must acknowledge that cyber criminals who take advantage of security vulnerabilities and abuse technology should be top of the list.

Ethical dilemmas

A fundamental element of the people part of cyber security is that of ethics. We have already looked at this in terms of the ethical considerations of security testing, but there are of course other dimensions to explore. To explore the ethical dilemmas of cyber security, let's work through three scenarios as a thought exercise (my thoughts on each are included after the last scenario).

SCENARIO ONE: RANSOMWARE IN A HOSPITAL
You are the chief information security officer of a hospital. Your phone rings and you are informed that all computers in the hospital have been locked down by ransomware. No one in the hospital can access any data, which means the ability of the hospital to continue operating is going to be severely impacted. This could, of course, seriously affect patients' health. What

ethical considerations must you consider when trying to decide whether to pay the ransom?

SCENARIO TWO: TROLL-HUNTING

You work as a social engineer. Your partner is being targeted online by a troll, who is bullying them and causing upset. Through open-source intelligence (OSINT) you believe that you have identified the troll in real life, finding various email addresses and social media profiles for them, including ones that they seem to have attempted to keep separate from their troll persona. Do you use your skills to hack their accounts and look for further information you could use to stop them attacking your partner?

SCENARIO THREE: BUG REPORTING

You are an ethical hacker. Whilst using the internet, you identify what you believe may be a bug in a website, which you are concerned could enable someone malicious to access the personal information of people who have an account with the site. You contact the site and report the vulnerability but receive no reply. A month later, you try again; this time when you receive no reply you turn to Twitter. You tweet the company and say you have found a bug but don't provide details publicly. This prompts a reply, but when you privately explain your findings, the organization say that they are not concerned about the vulnerability and they don't believe it could have the impact that you think it could have. Do you disclose details of what you have found publicly?

When it comes to ethical dilemmas, there is not necessarily a clear-cut answer. This is what makes them a dilemma, or ethical paradox, because if it was clear what was the right thing to do, there would be no cause for debate. However, I wanted to share my thoughts on the scenarios I have outlined so you can compare them with your own and see whether there was anything you or I missed.

MY THOUGHTS ON SCENARIO ONE

Threats to people's physical health, potentially their lives, should surely be our paramount consideration. Therefore, a strong ethical argument can be made for paying the ransom in this case. Nevertheless, paying the ransom poses some problems:

- There is no guarantee the criminals will honour their word (they are criminals after all...) and provide you with the decrypt key, in which case you will be no further forward but hospital funds will have been wasted.
- More than wasted, hospital funds will have been transferred to criminals, funding further criminal endeavour.
- In paying the ransom, you may have potentially marked the hospital as a weak target and made it a more likely future target.

MY THOUGHTS ON SCENARIO TWO

Do two wrongs make a right? This scenario does not just raise ethical questions, it also centres on questions of legalities. If you hack their accounts you are, of course, breaking the law. There are many other options you could pursue, not least of which would be to take the information you have gathered to the police, combined with evidence of the bullying and harassment that has been levelled at your partner.

MY THOUGHTS ON SCENARIO THREE

Responsible disclosure is a subject of frequent debate in cyber security. What is the ethical approach to take here? If you publicly report the bug, you are potentially making the vulnerability widely known and therefore opening up the potential for criminals to use information you have supplied to carry out an attack. On the other hand, criminals may already be aware of the vulnerability and could be actively exploiting it. You have tried to privately alert the organization to no avail. By publicly exposing the vulnerability, the weight of the security community could help pressure the organization into addressing an issue that you believe is putting people's personal data at risk.

OWASP provide a cheat-sheet to help people report vulnerabilities in a responsible manner, which outlines a way to progress a report if the organization is being unresponsive. This includes keeping good documentation of your work and steps taken, alerting trusted third parties such as National CERT (Computer Emergency Response Team) or data privacy regulators, and taking an approach which encourages trust, transparency and openness.[10]

Destruction

In the lifecycle of technology and data, and how people are central to security considerations, we must not overlook the importance of how data is deleted and technology is destroyed. This can be as simple, and personal, as what an individual does with their old mobile phone when they buy a new one, through to the more complicated issues of how large organizations delete data in a timely and secure manner and how they dispose of hardware when it is no longer required.

Software can be used to overwrite data. There are many different government and industry standards that relate to software-based overwriting, with the aim of ensuring that it is carried out to a sufficient standard. Like every stage of the life-cycle, secure data destruction relies on the human element to consider the importance of what they are doing in relation to the impact it could have on information security. And, like every other stage, there is the danger of malicious action when it comes to data destruction. This can include malicious actors accessing and abusing data that the data owner failed to adequately destroy as well as the malicious destruction of data. A sobering example of malicious data destruction is included in Chapter 10, which outlines the cyber attack experienced by the shipping giant Maersk in 2018.

This chapter has provided an overview of many of the ways in which people are fundamental to cyber security. In the next chapter, we will look at another fundamentally human part of cyber security: social engineering, and how people are manipulated by criminals. We will look at the evolution of social engineering to understand some of the latest scams and what makes us, as human beings, so susceptible to them.

Notes

1   National Cyber Security Centre (2018) Secure by Default, National Cyber Security Centre, 7 March, www.ncsc.gov.uk/information/secure-default (archived at https://perma.cc/B2SA-ACPJ)
2   Symantec (2019) Internet security threat report, volume 24, www.symantec.com/content/dam/symantec/docs/reports/istr-24-2019-en.pdf (archived at https://perma.cc/U6ER-C8PL)
3   https://www.vpnmentor.com/blog/report-ghana-nss-leak/ (archived at https://perma.cc/GJ2C-3U4K)
4   https://www.darkreading.com/application-security/cloud-misconfig-exposes-3tb-sensitive-airport-data-amazon-s3-bucket (archived at https://perma.cc/L65N-3GNJ)
5   https://www.theregister.com/2022/12/20/mcgraw_hills_s3_buckets_exposed/ (archived at https://perma.cc/L7CQ-4NQT)
6   Wright, M and Horton, H (2019) Bank customers lose £9.1 million in five years to 'sim swap' scams, Telegraph, 30 November, www.telegraph.co.uk/news/2019/11/30/bank-customers-lose-91-million-five-years-sim-swap-scams (archived at https://perma.cc/9CLX-629U)
7   Graff, G (2017) How a dorm room Minecraft scam brought down the internet, Wired, 13 December, www.wired.com/story/mirai-botnet-minecraft-scam-brought-down-the-internet (archived at https://perma.cc/EU5H-P5KH)
8   Hilton, S (2016) Dyn analysis summary of Friday October 21 attack (blog), Dyn, 26 October, https://dyn.com/blog/dyn-analysis-summary-of-friday-october-21-attack (archived at https://perma.cc/RF7S-SJ5N)

9 Ragan, S (2016) Here are the 61 passwords that powered the Mirai IoT botnet, CSO Online, 3 October, www.csoonline.com/article/3126924/here-are-the-61-passwords-that-powered-the-mirai-iot-botnet.html (archived at https://perma.cc/TV66-VHK4)
10 OWASP (no date) Vulnerability disclosure cheat sheet, OWASP Cheat Sheet series, https://cheatsheetseries.owasp.org/cheatsheets/Vulnerability_Disclosure_Cheat_Sheet.html (archived at https://perma.cc/39FZ-5UVS)

CHAPTER FIVE

Social engineering

For decades, the cyber security industry (before it was even called cyber security; when it was IT security, information assurance, information security or infosec) focused heavily on the technical side of attack and defence. Arguably, it still does. Cybercriminals have taken this for the opportunity that it was, and focused on targeting people rather than technology as a means of gaining access to an organization, to information, to money. This is social engineering: the manipulation of people in order to gain access to information, assets or money that the target would not or should not ordinarily give.

Social engineering red flags

Social engineering attacks utilize common psychological tricks to manipulate targets. By playing on the emotional responses of targets, social engineers know that their victims are not thinking clearly; emotion clouds our judgement and we are more likely to react impulsively. Common features of social engineering attacks, the red flags that we can look out for, include:

- the attacker eliciting sympathy from their target;
- flattery;
- the need for secrecy;
- the attacker engineering a sense of closeness with their target;
- the attacker making their target feel ashamed;
- time pressure/a sense of urgency;
- the attacker exerting authority over their target.

Social engineering is now firmly associated with cyber security, but the concept has been around for much longer than computers. People using psychological tricks to fool others into giving them money, information or access has probably been happening as long as humankind has been in existence.

Non-criminal social engineering

We see many examples of social engineering in our everyday lives. A car salesperson may put the price of a vehicle higher than a customer will pay, and then allow the customer to negotiate them down, so the customer feels they have been clever enough to get a discount – even if the price they end up paying is higher than any price they had originally planned on. Politicians pose with babies during election campaigns. Some PR campaigns are so bad that we share them on social media, not realizing we are playing into the hands of the campaign designers, who understand that 'no publicity is bad publicity'.

There are also increasing opportunities within the field of cyber security to work as a social engineer, or at least to perform social engineering tests of organizations as one part of a career. Somebody working as an ethical and legal social engineer will test the human and, often, physical defences of an organization in a similar way to how a penetration tester will test the digital defences. It's not something I do regularly, but I have performed social engineering tests for organizations myself. One was a hospital; the brief was to attempt to get to the most sensitive parts of the hospital – the data centres and the executive offices. The scope of a social engineering test is really important, much like the scope of a pen test. It was imperative in the hospital test, for example, that we did not interfere with patient areas. This highlights one of many ways that ethics are so important in the field of cyber security: if we had acted without consideration of the scope of the test or without respect for professional ethics, we could have impacted on the proper running of the hospital and, ultimately, patient care.

Some social engineering tests may involve physically 'breaking in' to buildings. Others, like the hospital test, will centre on manipulating people to provide access to a building, system or information.

Why social engineering works

Social engineering works by taking advantage of human bias. It exploits people operating on autopilot, being 'mindless', being busy, being trusting and, ultimately, being human. After years of experience dealing with the fall-out of criminal social engineering attacks and helping organizations bolster their defences against these, I believe we can explain why someone is so susceptible to social engineering attacks by looking to behavioural economics, psychology and neuroscience. Too often, I hear people in the cyber security industry refer to someone clicking a malicious link as 'stupid', claiming 'users are the weakest link'. This is a very short-sighted and uninformed view and I hope it will soon be widely recognized as the outdated and unhelpful narrative that it is.

Instead, when someone is coerced into giving away sensitive information to an imposter on the phone, clicks a malicious link in an SMS text or downloads an attachment in a phishing email, we should understand that they do so for many reasons. Telling someone to avoid clicking links in suspicious emails is impossible advice and actually hinders more than it helps our attempts to help people defend themselves against social engineering. Many people simply *have* to click links and open attachments in emails all day long; how are they meant to recognize a suspicious email? Especially when spear-phishing emails have become so much more convincing in recent years. Giving people advice that fails to take into account their work requirements, and that is virtually impossible for anyone connected to the internet to follow, makes cyber security off-putting.

If we reject the lazy narrative that people who fall victim to social engineering attacks do so because they are 'stupid', then how can we better understand what actually makes us so susceptible to social engineering attacks?

Let's use a fictional case study (based on a real incident involving one of my clients) to look at this in more detail.

CASE STUDY   Alice and Bob

Bob works as a finance administrator in a manufacturing business, and a core part of his job is paying invoices, often for large sums of money. One Tuesday afternoon, Bob receives an email that looks like it comes from Alice, the company's CEO (red flag: authority). In the email, Alice tells Bob that she needs his help with a sensitive matter. The company are acquiring another business and Alice needs Bob to make an immediate transfer of £75,000 to secure the acquisition. It must be done immediately or there is a risk of the sale not going through (red flag: time pressure). It also must be kept confidential; in the email, Alice tells Bob that he must not tell any of his colleagues about this transaction as the acquisition is not publicly known, and if it became public knowledge it could impact the share price (red flag: the need for confidentiality). Alice ends the email by telling Bob 'I know I can rely on you to do this for us' (red flag: flattery). Bob feels the pressure of authority coming from his boss and his ego is flattered, being trusted with this important and confidential task. He does not question the story, which seems plausible, along with the need to keep the details to himself. He transfers the money without question.

FIGURE 5.1   Alice and Bob's email

From: Alice<mailto:CEO@yourcompany.com>
Sent: Wednesday, September 12, 2018 4:11:01 PM
To: Bob <Bob@yourcompany.com>
Subject: Confidential

Bob,

I need your help with something very sensitive. We are acquiring Malicious Media Inc. which has been kept extremely confidential because of the implications on the stock price. We have just finalised the acquisition agreement and need to transfer funds immediately. Please transfer £75,000 to the following account:

Bank: Big Bank
Name: Malicious Media
Acct Number: 12345678
Sort Code: 12-34-56

This acquisition is crucial to our business and it is imperative that this transfer of funds takes place at the utmost speed and with total discretion. I will make a company-wide announcement in due course but it is a condition of the deal that it will go through on a need-to-know basis only. I know that I can rely on you to do this for us.

Regards,
Alice

As soon as the transfer has gone through, Bob feels a sense of dread start to grow in the pit of his stomach. He breaks out in a cold sweat as he suddenly begins to question whether he did the right thing. He picks up the phone and calls the CEO's office, anxious to hear that the email was legitimate… but the CEO knows nothing of the email. She did not send it, and there is no such acquisition taking place.

Bob, Alice and the company have become victims of what is sometimes called CEO fraud – also called business email compromise (BEC) – and, unfortunately, it is too late to stop the transfer or get the money back.

So, what happened here? Why are we, as humans, so susceptible to social engineering attacks? Well, they work not because the people who fall victim to them are stupid, but because they take advantage of deep-rooted human bias. If it was stupidity at the root, then how do we explain Bob's sudden realization that the email was perhaps a scam, in the example above? But, likewise, if he recognized the email was most likely a spear-phish after he had transferred the money, why did he not realize a few seconds earlier, before it was too late and the transfer was made?

What interests me about this is that split second between Bob transferring the money (or it could be clicking the link, downloading the attachment, entering their username and password) and then realizing that all, perhaps, was not as it seemed. This is the same person, with the same level of intelligence, experience and training in one moment to the next. Their external environment is unlikely to have changed much, the office will likely be as noisy and busy after they have responded to the email as it was when they received it. This suggests that the influencing factors in social engineering are not the victim's level of intelligence, but rather the tactics of the attacker.

Hot states

We can turn to behavioural economics to understand what happens in Bob's brain to make him process the email automatically, and only question its validity once the transfer has been made. *Thinking, Fast and Slow* explains two ways of thinking.[1] The concept is also explored by Thaler and Sunstein in *Nudge*.[2] This work has been so influential that Richard Thaler won the Nobel Prize for economics in 2017 for his contribution to the field of behavioural economics. In *Nudge*, the authors refer to two ways of processing information in our brains, which they refer to as the Homer Simpson and the Spock ways of thinking. When we're processing information predominantly with the Homer way of thinking, we are impulsive, emotionally driven and short-termist: we do not consider the possible unintended consequences of our actions. On the other hand, when we're predominantly processing information with the Spock way of thinking, we are considered, cautious, rational and forward-thinking: we weigh up many possible outcomes of our actions. The Homer way of processing information is more likely to dominate when we are in what Thaler and Sunstein refer to as a 'hot state' and it is my observation that this is what social engineering does: it puts people into 'hot states'.[3] How does it do that? By using well-known triggers – the red flags we have seen referenced throughout the social engineering examples in this chapter, including authority, time pressure, the need for confidentiality and flattery (as in the example with Alice and Bob above), as well as temptation, appeals to sympathy, shame and many more.

HOT STATE EMAILS: SHAME

In 2018 and 2019, a huge number of people received spear-phishing emails that took advantage of the 'hot state' of shame. In pretty much every awareness-raising session I delivered for clients from mid-2018 to the time of writing in late 2019, someone told me they had received one of these emails. People have often been incredibly distressed by the email, losing sleep and even, in some cases, considering what they will do when the fallout of the email forces them to resign from their job.

This email begins by saying something along the lines of 'I know a secret about you, I know your password and it is [*password*]'. The password that is included is one that the victim either uses currently or has used in the past, which of course immediately captures their attention, and often terrifies them. This stranger knows their password! It also lays the foundation for the scam that follows: when you are manipulating someone, if you start with a truth then they are more likely to believe the lies that follow. So, having warmed the target up, the email continues. It says that the sender knows the recipient's password because the recipient was watching pornography on the internet, and in doing so exposed their computer to malicious software that enabled the sender to access all of their data (including passwords) and to spy on them. The email says that the sender has taken compromising, intimate footage of the recipient watching pornography, and they will release this footage to the recipient's friends and family if they do not pay a ransom, usually in bitcoin. Some variants of this spear-phishing email say that the pornography that the target was watching featured people who are under age and threatens to report the target to law enforcement if the ransom is not paid.

So, what's really happening? Well, the password at the start of the email was a truth, but the rest is lies. The sender did not get the password from spying on the recipient via malware. The sender got the password from a password dump. Over recent years, many companies have had their security breached and details of people's email addresses, passwords and other data stolen. When this happens, these files often end up being posted online and/or shared on the dark web. So, the criminals sending these spear-phishing emails are simply using email addresses and passwords from one of these breaches, or password dumps, to contact large numbers of people with targeted emails including the password associated with the email address, to attempt to extort money out of them by scaring and shaming them. Most people who receive these emails do not consider that the password came from a password dump; they may have heard of passwords being stolen when LinkedIn, MySpace or Yahoo (or one of the many, many others) were breached, but they don't put two and two together (and why would they?!). They also probably don't put two and two together because they are scared and ashamed. Maybe they had been watching pornography online, maybe they hadn't; when it comes to this scam it really doesn't matter, although the attackers are relying on the likelihood that enough recipients will have looked at pornography online at some point and that they will be reluctant to admit this to anyone, and risk compromising footage of themselves being made public. The criminals make the ransom amount purposefully low. They know that a lower ransom is more likely to be paid and so they target lots of people, demanding a low enough amount that a

THE HUMAN SIDE OF CYBER SECURITY

significant number of people will pay. Of course, when we pay a ransom like this, we are funding the continuation of cybercrime and encouraging the criminals to continue targeting other people (and probably ensuring that we are put on a list of victims who the criminals know have paid once, and are likely to pay again).

Researches at Malwarebytes looked into a spear-phishing email campaign similar to the one I describe above and calculated how much money the scam generated for the criminals behind it. They found that one campaign, most active between 1 February and 13 March 2019 (so, for approximately six weeks), collected a total of 21.6847451 bitcoins, which was a little over US $220,000 at the exchange rates at the time Malwarebytes did their analysis.[4] This is one campaign amongst many, which shows the scale of the problem we are currently facing.

Sextortion

As we've seen, social engineering manipulates the emotions and instincts of people to take advantage of them. If the target also feels ashamed or embarrassed, as in the case of the password/pornography email scam, then attackers know that they are also more likely to keep quiet about what is happening, which means the scam is more likely to be successful and less likely to be reported to law enforcement.

Another type of attack that takes advantage of this phenomenon is called online sexual coercion and extortion, commonly known as 'sextortion'. Sextortion attacks take many forms, but one of the most frequent takes place over social media.

Here's how it works: the target, who we'll call Sam, receives a friendship or connection request from somebody who they don't know, but who they feel inclined to get to know – let's call them Alex. Alex looks like an attractive person, with the usual personal information, likes and interactions that most profiles have. Sam accepts the request, because – why not? They're flattered, tempted, intrigued and keen to make a connection with this attractive person. Having made a connection, they develop an online relationship and Alex sends more and more pictures of themselves, including ones where they take their clothes off. Perhaps even some video footage. Alex asks for the same in return from Sam. Sam feels the pressure of temptation and reciprocity: Alex has done something for Sam and so Sam feels obliged to return the favour.

Reciprocity is why salespeople will offer customers a drink when they enter a car showroom. It can be argued that the human instinct to return a favour is hard-wired into our evolutionary development, as before we had money to buy goods and services, we traded based on reciprocity. Therefore, if someone does us a favour, we feel obliged to return the favour and we feel uncomfortable until we are even.

And so, this combination of temptation and reciprocity encourages Sam to send explicit pictures or video footage of themselves to Alex. At this point, unfortunately, Sam discovers that Alex is not who they seemed. Once the explicit images have been sent, Sam receives an extortion demand, requesting payment (usually by bitcoin, money transfer or by providing credit card details) and threatening that, if Sam doesn't pay up, the images will be released on the internet and sent to Sam's friends and family.

Many people quietly pay the ransom. Some do not, and never hear from the criminals behind the scam again. Some pay once and receive a second, then a third ransom message. Some victims are targeted not for money, but for more explicit photographs or videos. In 2021, reports of sextortion cases in the UK nearly doubled from 593 in 2020 to 1124, with 88 per cent of cases involving a male victim. In 80 per cent of cases, the perpetrators were criminal gangs, with 11 per cent carried out by current or former partners.[5] Unfortunately, we can be confident that the reported number of sextortion cases is only the tip of the iceberg, as many victims do not report the crimes to law enforcement (which the criminals are of course relying upon).[6]

It is understandable why people pay the ransom, or send the photographs being demanded, in return for the promise that the compromising photos or footage will be deleted. However, as with all ransom scenarios, we are dealing with criminals: the people behind these attacks cannot be trusted to keep their word. And, paying the ransom funds more criminal activity and encourages the continuation of these crimes. Ideally, none of us would ever be taken in by these social engineering attacks. Unfortunately, they are getting more sophisticated and we are only human. The good news is that awareness of social engineering is higher than ever, and as more people become attuned to the common type of attacks and the human emotions they take advantage of, the less successful these common attacks will be.

If you become a victim of a social engineering attack, whether sextortion or otherwise, the best thing to do is report it to law enforcement. When it comes to sextortion, many police forces now have direct experience of working with victims and have received specialist training not only in how to investigate or report the crimes, but also in how to be sensitive to the victim.

EXERCISE 5.1   Hot state triggers

Here's an example of an email. Read it carefully, and try to spot any 'hot state triggers' – words or phrases that could be red flags for a social engineering attack. Are there any other issues that should be investigated in this example?

Hi Sally

I've just landed in the States. We need to pay a supplier an overdue invoice, it's urgent and must be paid ASAP. I need you to keep this confidential – I can't go through the usual processes because there is an issue with fraud internally. I'm trusting you to do this quickly and to keep it quiet. I know I can rely on you.

Thanks

Phil

See the answer in the Appendix (page 244).

Notes

1   Khaneman, D (2011) *Thinking, Fast and Slow*, Farrar, Straus and Giroux, New York
2   Thaler, R and Sunstein, C (2008) *Nudge: Improving decisions about health, wealth, and happiness*, Yale University Press, New Haven
3   Thaler, R and Sunstein, C (2008) *Nudge: Improving decisions about health, wealth, and happiness*, Yale University Press, New Haven
4   Threat Intelligence Team (2019) The lucrative business of Bitcoin sextortion scams (updated) (blog), Malwarebytes Labs, 22 August, https://blog.malwarebytes.com/scams/2019/08/the-lucrative-business-of-bitcoin-sextortion-scams (archived at https://perma.cc/3NZH-5F73)
5   Coker, J (2022) UK Sextortion Cases Doubled in 2021, *Infosecurity Magazine*, 20 May. www.infosecurity-magazine.com/news/uk-sextortion-cases-doubled (archived at https://perma.cc/2FNG-6XT3)
6   National Crime Agency (no date) Record numbers of UK men fall victim to sextortion gangs (blog), NCA News, https://nationalcrimeagency.gov.uk/news/record-numbers-of-uk-men-fall-victim-to-sextortion-gangs (archived at https://perma.cc/M9PS-66NH)

CHAPTER SIX

Attacks that utilize social engineering

Phishing

When we consider social engineering attacks, phishing emails are a great place to start, partly because they are the most common (albeit far from the only) form of social engineering.[1] Phishing emails masquerade as coming from a legitimate source (such as a bank) and try to coerce the recipient into actions such as clicking a link, downloading an attachment, sending money or inputting your credentials. Phishing emails look like they come from a legitimate source, but they do not. For example, the email may look like it comes from a social media platform, such as LinkedIn, Twitter or Facebook, and contains a link to 'reset your password' or 'view messages'. When you click the link, a couple of things might happen: you might unwittingly download malware onto your device; or you might open a page, which again may look legitimate, and be prompted to input your credentials. So, in the example above, you could open a page that looks identical to the Facebook login page, but is in fact a fake page being run by cybercriminals. If you put your username and password into that page, you are handing them over to the criminals that run the page. There are many, many different examples of phishing emails: this is just one.

Spear-phishing

When many people think of phishing emails, they think of a now well-established scam in which an email comes from someone pretending to be a foreign prince, stating they have come into an unexpected source of wealth and they would like to share it with the recipient, if only the recipient would transfer a relatively small sum of money to make that possible. Phishing emails have evolved greatly from this scam, and many of the most successful phishing emails can now be more accurately categorized as spear-phishing emails, meaning they are targeted. They may use the recipient's name in the email, they may purport to come from the target's actual bank, or boss, or best friend. Some spear-phishing emails target people in the process of buying a house, coming from criminals who pose as the solicitor requesting the deposit be paid using new bank details. As we covered in the last chapter, some even contain reference to an internet password that the target uses or has used. Spear-phishing emails are unfortunately far more likely to be successful than standard phishing emails and, because of this, they have grown in volume phenomenally over the last few years. In fact, spear-phishing emails represent one of the most common ways in which organizations are compromised. This is partly because they have a high success rate, and partly because they can be used as a vehicle to carry out a number of attacks, from fraud to credential compromise to ransomware.

The targeted nature of spear-phishing emails is a core element in their success. Using a target's name, appearing to be sent from their boss, their bank, including their passwords – this all lends the emails an air of legitimacy, it makes them believable. We have become much more savvy to general phishing emails, but spear-phishing emails are, unfortunately, more likely to take us in.

However, as we saw in Chapter 5, we have seen a huge rise in awareness of emails that use social engineering techniques. An important factor in this growing awareness is the actions of many large organizations: because they are seeing so many attacks of this nature come in, and often have dealt with the fallout of what happens when the attacks are successful, they are spending effort, time and resource to make sure people are aware of the risks. As more people understand spear-phishing emails, and fewer people click on the links, download the attachments or transfer the money, the criminals change their methods. They move from emails to phone calls, social media, and messaging platforms such as WhatsApp.

Voice-phishing or vishing

Social engineering over the telephone is sometimes called vishing (voice phishing). Just like email spear-phishing, voice phishing calls are used by criminals for all sorts of malicious purposes. Let's look at one fictional scenario.

CASE STUDY Bill

Bill works in procurement for a large law firm. One day he receives a call from a woman who introduces herself as Catherine; she works for a paper supplier and would like to speak to someone about the possibility of supplying paper to the company. As Bill starts to fob Catherine off, a baby starts crying in the background and Catherine apologizes profusely, explaining she is a new mother trying to juggle work and being a new parent. What a coincidence! Bill is a new parent too, it's his first week back after paternity leave and he, too, is sleep deprived and trying to work out how to balance this new phase of life.

Catherine says how grateful she is that Bill understands, she gets a little choked up and divulges that, actually, she's not been making anywhere near as many sales since getting back to work after maternity leave. She explains that Bill will be doing her a huge favour if he just agrees to receive an email from her with some sales materials attached. If he opens the attachments on the email, that will increase her numbers just enough to get her boss off her back. Of course, Bill agrees and, when the email comes in, he is keen to help his new acquaintance out. He opens the email, he opens the attachments, but it just loads as some gobbledegook. He emails Catherine to let her know, but she doesn't reply and he is busy balancing work and parenthood, so he soon forgets. Unbeknown to Bill, the document he opened was embedded with malware which enabled criminals' access to the organization's network.

What Bill didn't realize is that the phone call was a ruse and the 'coincidence' of one new parent empathizing with another was no coincidence at all, but was a cover created by the criminals behind the scam. They saw Bill's twitter status about becoming a new dad, having already discovered via LinkedIn that he was in the perfect position in the law firm they wanted to target. Working in procurement, the criminals knew that Bill would receive lots of emails from suppliers and potential suppliers. They also knew that, working for a large law firm, Bill would have probably received cyber security training that warned him not to click on links or open attachments in emails he wasn't expecting. So, a simple phone call in advance, with a play on Bill's sympathy by using the background soundtrack of a baby crying, makes the scam more likely to succeed.

Voice phishing calls are sometimes used by criminals in the way described above, to warm targets up to the real attack, which might be in the form of an email. They are also used as the primary means of attack. For example, you may receive a call from someone who claims to be calling from your bank's fraud department and just needs some information from you to investigate suspicious activity on your account. The call may even show your bank's name on caller ID. However, if the caller starts asking for your PIN or password, that's a sign that they're certainly not calling from your bank. If I receive a call from my bank and the caller asks information of me, I always hang up and call a number that I know is valid (from the back of my bank card or statement).

The scenario with Bill illustrates that, as we become more aware of what the cyber criminals are doing, they change their methods in an attempt to evade detection. This is inevitable and, unfortunately, all part of the cat-and-mouse game between criminals and those who seek to defend against criminal activity. The more we raise awareness of spear-phishing emails and train people to resist them, the more (some) criminals will seek other ways to socially engineer us (particularly if they have a specific target). Any method of communication can be, and is, taken advantage of by social engineers. We see attacks not just over email and over the telephone, but also in person, via written letters, via SMS text messages and, of course, over social media and messaging apps such as WhatsApp.

CASE STUDY   Janessa Brazil

Will the real Janessa Brazil please stand up?

She is allegedly the most impersonated woman in the world, and there are apparently 100,000 online accounts using the images of Janessa Brazil, an adult entertainment star. The people running these accounts pose as various women to run romance scams, where they play a long game of convincing men that they are in a meaningful relationship and scam money from their victims. They 'catfish' their victims, using a (literal) playbook of scam tactics to run fake online profiles fronted by images of real women to trick men out of money.

In the podcast *Love, Janessa* the journalist Hannah Ajala goes in search of the woman behind the catfish pictures, Janessa Brazil herself. As part of the investigation, Ajala speaks with numerous men who believed they were in relationships with Janessa (or a woman by another name), some of whom have sent tens – even hundreds – of thousands of dollars to the scammers operating under the guise of Janessa. For example, there is Roberto, a self-employed sustainable farmer from Sardinia. Roberto believed he was in a loving and committed online relationship with a woman named Hanna for four years. Over the course of their 'relationship', Roberto estimates that he sent 'Hanna' $250,000. When he ran out of funds, the relationship ended.[2]

Romance scams exploit people who are in search of a relationship or companionship, taking advantage of people who are lonely or looking for love. This explains why there was a rise in romance scams in 2020. With so many restrictions on our physical lives due to the Covid-19 pandemic, many people searched for greater online connectivity. While digital connectivity offered so many benefits during this time (and continues to do so), it was also exploited by cybercriminals. In the UK, data suggests there was a 20 per cent increase in bank transfer romance fraud in 2020 compared to 2019, with the total value of these scams rising by 12 per cent to £18.5 million.[3] These are only the cases we know of, so unfortunately the number of victims and amount of money lost is likely to be higher.

The scammers running romance fraud often spend months building the relationships with their targets, love bombing them with attention and flattery, before asking for money. They may elicit sympathy from their victims and convince them that they need money for an emergency, such as medical bills. They sometimes play on the hope of their target, saying that the money is for a flight to finally see them in person. The victims, then, are susceptible to sunk cost fallacy, reluctant to abandon the relationship because by that point they have invested a great deal of time and attention to it. Confirmation bias also plays its part, with victims interpreting any ambiguous information as confirming their belief that the relationship is real. Finally, of course, these scams work because victims are being manipulated by trained, experienced, professional criminals. With their playbook of tactics, the scammers use flattery, sympathy, attention, and many more manipulative techniques to build up relationships that – to the victims – feel very much like reality.

There is often a psychological impact on victims of social engineering and fraud. Research has found that victims of identity theft experience emotional and physical symptoms. The financial impact can be devastating. The psychological impact can be even more cruel. Victims of romance scams experience a 'double-hit': they have both a financial loss and the loss of a relationship. Victims can be traumatized, even experiencing post-traumatic stress symptoms, describing the loss as like a 'death' and – in some cases – victims report contemplating suicide.[4] Victims can feel ashamed, and this can be reinforced by the attitude of friends, family and wider society.

Romance scams remind us of the need to root our approach to cyber security in empathy and compassion. The more we victim blame, the more people attach a sense of shame to becoming a victim. The more people feel ashamed, the less they will engage with what we have to say. The less people engage with our messages, the less they know about cyber security and the more potential there is for them to become a victim in future.[5]

We must also be aware that even in more closed communication forums, such as messaging services like WhatsApp, we can still be targeted with social engineering attacks. Let's take a look at another case study.

CASE STUDY WhatsApp Mum and Dad scam

Let's imagine it's Friday afternoon and you get a WhatsApp. It's not a number you know but you quickly learn it's from a family member and they need your help. They start with something like 'Hi Mum' or 'Hi Dad' and explain that their phone is broken and this is a new phone or one they have borrowed. You exchange some messages and chat for a while. Then they ask if you can help them. They have a bill to pay. They might say that telephone banking isn't working on their new phone yet but if they don't pay the bill they'll face high interest or be in trouble,

They'll give you the bank account details and say they need you to pay perhaps around one or two thousand pounds.

And it's all a scam, known as the Mum and Dad scam. On average, victims are losing £1,950 each to this scam.[6] Sometimes, thankfully, the bank is able to identify the scam and block the transfer or refund the money. But sadly, not always.

Lloyds Bank have reported that WhatsApp scams increased 2000 per cent in 2021.[7] As we become more savvy to social engineering, criminals evolve their methods and channels. They also follow the numbers and with two billion people using WhatsApp, that's a lot of targets. Criminals often only need a small percentage of the people they target to transfer money, for them to profit.

This is a reminder (and something you may want to share with your family and friends) that if you receive a message from a loved one from a new number, and they say they need your help, call them on the original number that you have saved for them. If you can't get hold of them, ask yourself whether the messages look and sound like something your loved one would say. You could ask them a question only they could answer to verify if it's them. Finally, remember my golden rule for social engineering: be especially wary of any communication that is unexpected, makes you feel something and asks you to do something.

CASE STUDY   Covid 19 social engineering: Business email compromise
and beyond

The target may work for a large organization. They are targeted by a cyber criminal who could gain access to their email account in a number of ways: perhaps by cracking their password, if it is weak; by discovering that their password is the same one that they used for a service that failed to secure their users' passwords (such as LinkedIn in 2012 or Yahoo in 2013 and 2014 – not reported until 2016); or by sending them a spear-phishing email that encourages them to click on a link and input their credentials (perhaps the email would claim that someone has been trying to access their account and they need to put their username and password in to verify their identity). Once the criminal has accessed their email account, they use this access to send emails to their contacts requesting a transfer of money. These scams often target individuals working in the finance department of organizations and sectors where large transfers of money are common, for example estate agents and law firms. This is Business Email Compromise (BEC).

According to the FBI, there was a 65 per cent increase in BEC attacks from July 2019 to December 2021. The scam has been reported in all 50 states of the USA and 177 countries. The exposed dollar loss (both actual and attempted loss) totalled over $43 billion, rising from $10 billion in 2019. The FBI attribute the huge spike at least partly to the changing working practices that were brought about as a result of Covid-19.[8]

FIGURE 6.1   Reported loss associated with BEC/cryptocurrenct complaints

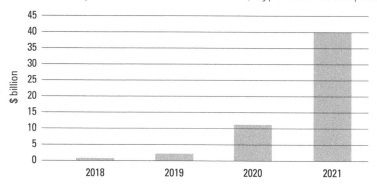

Source: FBI Public Service Announcement 24 May 2022

For most of us, Covid-19 was a crisis. For cybercriminals, it was an opportunity. Many organizations went through a forced digital transformation, accelerating changes to their working practices and technology infrastructure that may have been planned for the coming years, but suddenly had to be put in place in a matter of weeks – even days. This included moving to the cloud and transitioning large amounts of the workforce from office working to home working. Cyber criminals took advantage of Covid-19 in multiple ways, including launching attacks against rapidly deployed remote working infrastructure, BEC attacks that sought to exploit the more isolated working practices of people working from home, and using the pandemic as a lure in phishing emails, messages and phone calls.

The move to remote working, the stress and anxiety of the pandemic, the changing information landscape and the desire of many of us to know as much as we could about what was happening formed a perfect storm of social engineering. In the UK, the NCSC detected more UK government-branded scams relating to Covid-19 than any other subject.[9]

Money trails and cryptocurrency

The cases in the chapter so far describe scenarios in which the cyber criminals are trying to convince their targets in the UK to transfer money to bank accounts. We can assume that the money will be transferred via money mules and that, when it is withdrawn, it will most likely be done in countries where the UK does not have legal jurisdiction. Usually, by the time the organization realizes they have been a victim of fraud, informs law enforcement and there is an investigation, the money is gone. In some cases, following the money can lead to identification of the criminals.

The ability of law enforcement to (potentially) trace crimes through money trails has been a factor in the rise of ransomware: the rise of online ransomware can be tied to the emergence of cryptocurrency. Many ransomware attacks that seek to extort money from people do not ask for money transfers in the traditional sense, but rather demand payment in bitcoin or other digital currency. Only if the perpetrator is trying to appear legitimate will they ask for money to be transferred via a bank. Many people who mine, store and trade digital currency do so legitimately, but the relative anonymity that digital currency facilitates enables cyber criminals to extort money from people with much less chance of being identified than if they were using traditional currency.

Cryptocurrency – and the systems used to facilitate cryptocurrency earning, investment and exchange – are also a target of cybercriminals. In 2022, it was estimated that at least $1.4 billion was stolen in cyber attacks on cyptocurrency bridges alone.[10]

Bridges are software that enables someone to send tokens out of one blockchain (ledger) and receive them on a separate chain; essentially, they facilitate the exchange of cryptocurrency. The amount of money that flows through cryptocurrency bridges makes them an attractive target for cybercriminals, and security has been found to be lacking in many cases. In June 2022, the Harmony Horizon bridge was the target of a $100 million theft of cryptocurrency. Some of the accounts used to launder the assets were frozen and the FBI – and many others – concluded that the attack was the work of North Korea's Lazarus Group.

The biggest cryptocurrency cyber attack (to date) was reported in March 2022 when $615 million was stolen from Ronin Network, a platform powering the mobile game Axie Infinity. In the game, millions of players around the world fight animated characters called Axies to win cryptocurrency, and players can also exchange the digital coins they earn. Ronin Network found that the attack started in November 2021 when they loosened security controls to manage the growing userbase caused by their growing popularity.

Ransomware

'Ransomware is the most acute cyber threat facing the UK'
LINDY CAMERON, CEO NATIONAL CYBER SECURITY CENTRE (NCSC)

Picture this: a small business owner receives an email that looks as if it comes from the government, with the subject 'Your tax return'. The email states that there is important information in the attachment relating to the company's tax return, and that this must be completed and returned within 48 hours, or a fine will be issued.

The business owner, feeling under pressure, opens the attachment. The attachment contains no information. When the business owner closes the attachment and attempts to resume work, they discover that they cannot access any information. Their files are locked. A pop-up box appears on their screen informing them that their system has been infected, all of their data is encrypted and they must pay a ransom to receive the decrypt key and be able to access their data once again. The ransom will usually need to be paid in bitcoin, and sometimes the cyber criminals will be 'helpful' by including 'frequently asked questions' on what bitcoin is and how the target can get hold of some and make the transfer. This is ransomware by social engineering: malicious software that holds data to ransom.

The response to ransomware is a good example of collaboration in the cyber security community. The No More Ransom initiative was launched in July 2016 by law enforcement and cyber security companies (the founding partners were Europol, the Dutch Police, Kaspersky and McAfee; they have now been joined by many more law enforcement agencies, government agencies and cyber security companies). No More Ransom keeps a repository of decrypt keys and applications that can unlock data that has been encrypted by different kinds of data. When an individual or organization is affected by ransomware, they can visit www.nomoreransom.org to access decryption tools for many different types of ransomware.

Ransomware spreads in different ways, from social engineering to technical mechanisms (as we saw with WannaCry in Chapter 3). It impacts organizations of all sizes and all sectors.

We experienced a paradigm shift in ransomware in the years 2017–2019. Ransomware as a Service (RaaS) emerged, in which some criminal gangs run ransomware payloads which are then operated by 'partners' who pay for the use of the payload, bypassing their need for technical skill. At the same time, cybercriminals changed their strategies, moving away from targeting consumers with ransomware and focusing on attacking enterprises, enabling them to demand higher sums of money, for example:

- In May 2021, one of the largest US insurance firms CNA Financial reportedly paid $40 million to cyber criminals behind a ransomware attack in which data was also stolen.
- In January 2023, the UK Royal Mail experienced a ransomware attack which disrupted their operations for several days; the LockBit ransomware group claimed responsibility and published communications which showed the group demanding $79 million – and Royal Mail refusing to pay 'the absurd amount of money you have demanded'.[11]

In 2022, 18 ransomware incidents in the UK required a national response, including an attack on a water utility company, South Staffordshire Water.[12] In 2021, financial institutions in the US observed nearly $1.2 billion in costs associated with ransomware attacks in the US alone.[13] As well as businesses, hospitals and schools, local governments are increasingly impacted by ransomware attacks. In October 2020, Hackney Council in the UK suffered a ransomware attack, the impact of which was still being dealt with at the time of writing over two years later:

> People's health, housing situations, and finances suffered as a result of the insidious criminal group's attack. The attack against Hackney stands out not just because of its severity, but also the amount of time it has taken for the organization to recover and help people in need.[14]

It is understandable why organizations pay up, particularly if they have not backed up their data and feel their only hope of getting access to the data back is to pay the ransom. In some cases, losing the data could have serious business ramifications, putting profits – and jobs – on the line. However, there are many good reasons not to pay. Firstly, when you're the victim of a ransomware attack, you are negotiating with criminals, and although they may say that they will give you the decrypt key to access the data in return for payment, they may not stay true to their word. In addition, by paying the ransom, you are marking yourself as a target who will pay up, and so you may find that you become a more frequent target of cybercrime. In some cases, when victims pay the ransom, they are sent a discount code to use in future attacks. Finally, paying the ransom also supports the ransomware business model (telling criminals that it is a worthwhile thing to keep doing) and funds their activities, meaning they are more likely to continue doing what they are doing.

This is why the FBI does not support paying a ransom in response to ransomware, and why governments around the world are taking measures to crack down on the gangs behind these attacks. In February 2023, the UK and US governments took coordinated action to sanction seven Russian cyber criminals who are linked to the group behind the most damaging ransomware attacks in recent years. The UK National Crime Agency (NCA) found that the group behind the Trickbot, Conti and RYUK ransomware strains has extorted at least £27 million from 149 UK victims across the public and private sectors.[15] As part of the sanctions, the seven cybercriminals had assets frozen and travel bans imposed upon them, alongside a reminder to organizations that:

> Making funds available to the individuals such as paying
> ransomware, including in crypto assets, is prohibited under these
> sanctions. Organizations should have or should put in place robust
> cyber security and incident management systems to prevent and
> manage serious cyber incidents.[16]

When it comes to ransomware, prevention is incredibly important and the best advice is to keep offline backups of data (online backups can be infected with ransomware themselves), test the backups to make sure they are working as you would expect, keep devices and systems patched and up to date, and raise awareness of social engineering. Technical defences against phishing emails are key (including filtering and network segmentation), as phishing emails are increasingly sophisticated and expecting individuals to always be able to identify phishing emails is unrealistic. Likewise, it is vital that organizations build a cyber security culture in which people understand the importance of reporting phishing emails and feel safe that they can do so without fearing becoming the scapegoat. The right phish at the wrong time can catch us all.

Offline social engineering attacks

The social engineering attacks discussed in this chapter so far have focused on social engineering via digital methods. The rise in connectibility offered by the internet has been undoubtedly positive in a great many ways, but one of the unfortunate side-effects has been the opportunity it has offered cyber criminals for scamming people and organizations. However, we must remember that social engineering does not just take place over technology, but can be, and is, carried out in person.

In 2017, a man walked into a bank in Malaysia wearing a t-shirt, Bermuda shorts and flip-flops, carrying a backpack. He had a piece of paper, apparently showing the bank's floor plan, and, after identifying himself as a fire extinguisher technician, he was refused entry to the bank's back office when he failed to show any identification. However, he calmly stood in wait and, when the opportunity presented itself, he snuck into the restricted area of the bank and 'checked' the fire extinguishers before making his way to the safe room. When a cashier entered the safe room, the man placed a magnet on the door to prevent it locking when the cashier left. When the coast was clear, he made his way into the safe room and filled his backpack with RM 600,000 ($143,000) in cash. On his way out of the bank, the man stopped for a calm chat with the security guard. It took a few hours before staff realized the cash was gone and, on reviewing the CCTV footage, were able to piece together what had happened.

This example shows that, even in this modern age, security does not stop at technology. Physical space is an important component of cyber security, which we will explore in more detail in the following chapter.

Notes

1 Caveat: I said that phishing emails are currently the most common form of social engineering. The operative word in that sentence is 'currently'. The more savvy we become to phishing emails (including spear-phishing, of course), the more cybercriminals will evolve their methods. By the time this book is published, the most common method of social engineering may be over social media or messaging apps such as WhatsApp.

2 Love, Janessa podcast

3 https://www.actionfraud.police.uk/fauxmance (archived at https://perma.cc/X4GY-MS2Z)

4 Whitty, MT and Buchanan, T (2016). The online dating romance scam: The psychological impact on victims – both financial and non-financial, *Criminology & Criminal Justice*, 16(2), 176–194. https://doi.org/10.1177/1748895815603773 (archived at https://perma.cc/9T4S-BGP5)

5 https://www.cygenta.co.uk/post/psychological-impact-phishing (archived at https://perma.cc/TD8F-Q4S6)

6 https://www.lloydsbankinggroup.com/assets/pdfs/media/press-releases/2022-press-releases/lloyds-bank/31.01.2022-whatsapp-scams-surge-over-200-per-cent-in-a-year.pdf (archived at https://perma.cc/Y5PU-KPTF)

7 ibid

8 https://www.ic3.gov/Media/Y2022/PSA220504 (archived at https://perma.cc/TWV3-FQXK)

9 https://www.ncsc.gov.uk/files/NCSC-Annual-Review-2022.pdf (archived at https://perma.cc/ZF9Q-ZCE4)

10 https://www.cnbc.com/2022/08/10/hackers-have-stolen-1point4-billion-this-year-using-crypto-bridges.html (archived at https://perma.cc/CJ57-QE4V)

11 https://www.theguardian.com/business/2023/feb/15/under-no-circumstances-will-we-pay-that-absurd-amount-royal-mail-tells-hackers (archived at https://perma.cc/A6ZT-RHSF)

12 NCSC 2022 annual report

13 https://www.fincen.gov/news/news-releases/fincen-analysis-reveals-ransomware-reporting-bsa-filings-increased-significantly (archived at https://perma.cc/PY4R-2VBY)

14 https://www.wired.co.uk/article/ransomware-attack-recovery-hackney
(archived at https://perma.cc/GV94-6Z85)

15 https://www.nationalcrimeagency.gov.uk/news/ransomware-criminals-
sanctioned-in-joint-uk-us-crackdown-on-international-cyber-crime (archived at
https://perma.cc/F53M-NVM5)

16 ibid

PART FOUR

The physical side of cyber security

CHAPTER SEVEN

Why physical space matters in cyber security

Physical space can sometimes be overlooked when it comes to cyber security. Given the importance of how people, technology and information converge in physical terms, this is an oversight. The security of information has always been paramount to individuals, organizations and nations, well before there was a cyber element to it, and the physical dimension remains just as crucial now – after all, digital security always has a physical dimension.

In December 2019, the building company Balfour Beatty had its contract to refurbish the headquarters of the UK's Secret Intelligence Service (SIS, better known as MI6) terminated after losing over 100 papers which provided details of the building layout and security measures.[1] This example highlights the importance of physical security, as the misplacement of paperwork – itself a physical asset – posed a threat to the physical security of a building that requires stringent security and protection. The information detailed on the plans could have enabled anyone with malicious intent, such as terrorists, to plan an attack on the building with insider knowledge of where alarms are situated and how to move around the building. Although most of the plans were recovered inside the building, the security oversight was deemed serious enough for the company responsible to be removed from the project.

Although this is an extreme example, relating to a building that requires the utmost security, physical security is important to all organizations. At an organizational level, the correct installation of physical security measures (which increasingly have a digital element to them) is vital in the protection of information. A fundamental part of physical security for a building is access control systems.

Access control systems

Systems to control physical access to information all fall under a very broad area that covers many mechanisms, from physical keys and simple passwords through to sophisticated biometric and multi-factor authentication (MFA) systems.

Almost every system in use today has flaws. Some are simple to bypass, and others require a much more concerted effort to attack. Four factors to assess the value of an access control system (ACS) are:

- whether it has been designed to provide the security level that is required;
- whether the system has been correctly installed;
- whether the system is user friendly (or so difficult to use that people find workarounds);
- the education of the end user.

Choosing proportionate security controls is also fundamentally important, because security measures that feel like overkill to people are more likely to be bypassed out of frustration. A retina scan might be perfect for protecting a server room but would certainly be overkill to restrict access to the office canteen. Selecting the best ACS comes back to understanding the asset(s) being protected in conjunction with the risks, threats, vulnerabilities and various mitigations on offer (as covered in Chapter 2).

As is so often the case with security, it's best not to rely on one single ACS, but rather to layer up multiple systems to make sure that a bypass of one control is caught by the other systems. Here are some common types of ACS that can work together in various situations.

Badges and lanyards

Access badges and lanyards are a ubiquitous access control feature in most organizations; however, once again, the execution of a system of badges and lanyards makes the difference between security theatre and an effective security control.

Badges are a short-range identification tool and lanyards are used for longer-range identification. To be effective:

- Badges need to be large enough and clear enough to show the bearer to be the person on the badge. They have to be identifiable from a short range and must be updated regularly.
- Lanyards need to be distinct.
- Badges and lanyards must be worn at all times on the site.
- Badges often have in-built access mechanisms, requiring a user to swipe or tap their badge to gain access to a building or area within a building; for this to be effective, the system cannot be allowed to be overridden by people tailgating, leaving doors propped open or being able to convince security to grant them access, for example because they are familiar.

It is common for these requirements to be overlooked. Badges are often overloaded with information and photos become outdated or worn out from use. Lanyards are often customized by their wearers, and whilst this allows wearers to express their identity, too many customized lanyards negate the reason for wearing one in the first place. Lanyards are like flags announcing to the room or building that you are part of the company; if everyone is wearing different colours or styles then that security advantage is undermined.

Another downside to both of these systems is when the wearer does not remove the badge and lanyard when they leave the building. This allows them to be identified, opening an opportunity for social engineering, and also enables an attacker to steal or replicate the badge if they are seeking access to the site.

Creating and maintaining a viable security system that utilizes badges and lanyards really comes down to the education of the people wearing them. People must be informed as to why they need to wear specific things, and when *not* to wear them, as well as the implications of both falling into the wrong hands.

Biometrics

In the face of many security issues associated with passwords, more and more manufacturers are moving towards using biometric access control systems. Like all security controls, biometric systems are not a silver bullet: they have benefits and drawbacks.

In areas where it might be possible to shoulder surf, overhear or otherwise clone or replicate a security measure (such as a password) being used, biometrics can come into their own, utilizing gait, hand spans, fingerprint or retinas to create a unique key for every individual. However, it is often easier than expected to bypass these systems, from using fake 3D printed faces through to easily lifting and cloning fingerprints. As the levels of sophistication of these systems grow, they all need an element of fuzziness in order to work. A facial recognition system still needs to work if the user grows a beard and a fingerprint system still needs to function if they cut their finger; there needs to be some level of identification to prevent an overwhelming number of false positives that lock out a user. This careful balance of identification versus lockout provides a weak point that can be exploited by criminals.

Magnetic locks

Magnetic locks (mag locks) can be found in most offices and institutional buildings. They are an incredible invention, taking the simple concept of the electromagnet and making it into an effective access control system that is simple to install and use. One large metal plate is affixed to the door and another to the door frame. One of these will have an electromagnet attached, which is a core of iron with wires wrapped around it. If electricity is flowing through the wires, this induces a magnetic field in the iron core; with this very strong magnetic field, it attracts the other metal plate to it, which keeps the door tightly shut. The door will be kept tightly shut until the flow of electricity is stopped (for example via a switch that is activated by pressing a button), breaking the magnetic induction and allowing the door to open.

As with any security system, mag locks need to be installed correctly – otherwise they are trivial to bypass. The two most common flaws in mag locks stem from flaws in the installation of the system itself. Magnetic locks are very strong, which can lead to people underestimating the size of lock they need for a door. Although they are very strong, the right size lock still needs to be used on a door; smaller locks can only handle about 10 pounds of pressure, so using a lock that is too small allows the door to be pulled or pushed open, overcoming the magnetic force and leaving the door intact.

Another extremely common installation flaw is when the magnetic part (where the electronics are mounted) is placed on the wrong side of the door – the public-facing, or unrestricted, part. This means that the controlling parts of the system are on

THE PHYSICAL SIDE OF CYBER SECURITY

the side an attacker can easily access – if a malicious actor knows to take advantage of this access, then your system can be easily compromised.

CCTV

At the organizational level, cameras are often installed to monitor people's activity, deter negative behaviours and capture footage of incidents – in theory. CCTV is often not part of an access control system but part of the physical monitoring of a building or estate. However, in practice, there are a number of issues that limit the value of CCTV, too often reducing it to security theatre.

Poor quality

CCTV cameras are often used just as a deterrent, but when required, the quality of CCTV images is of paramount importance. However, organizations often buy lower-budget cameras and fail to upgrade them, despite the fact that smaller, better-quality cameras are being produced every year that would be cheaper than a standard system installed a few years previously.

Lack of monitoring

As individuals, when we see a CCTV camera we often assume it is being monitored. Signs beside cameras will state that it is, and scenes from Hollywood movies reinforce the expectation, in which we see banks of monitors being constantly observed by two security guards who watch for every minor incident, person or bag that looks out of place. In reality, it is most common that the only 'person' watching CCTV output is in fact a recording device, sometimes one that records over the same tape as frequently as every few hours or days.

The common lack of active monitoring means that CCTV cameras are not active security measures, as often assumed, but rather part of a passive retrospective system, which highlights misgivings about the level of security that CCTV provides. Of course, there may be a need to have measures in place to capture evidence of crime being committed, but it is important that the role of CCTV at the organizational level has been determined and understood, with the CCTV system then configured to support that role. If it is decided and understood that CCTV is there to record activity, with recordings that will be retained for a set amount of time, there is no problem. If it is expected that CCTV will be an active security measure to identify suspicious behaviour in real-time, an approach which enables that to occur must be put in place. CCTV is a tool and, like all tools, has to be used effectively.

Poor placement and lack of coverage

These two issues are separate but related. The poor placement of a camera, actively monitored or not, is the difference between it being worthwhile having a system or not bothering with CCTV in the first place and using the money elsewhere. CCTV is a finite resource; you can only afford so many cameras and the placement of them is vital to make sure that the most sensitive areas are covered. Not only is the placement important but *how* they are placed really matters. Cameras should cover each other, they should have no blind spots and should not be placed at a height that is easily reachable by an attacker. Placement of cameras also needs to take into account weather conditions: if a camera is facing direct sunlight or is in direct heavy rain, it can be impossible to record anything of value. Any of these flaws in placement can allow a criminal to disrupt, move or otherwise disable the camera. This sounds obvious, but if you look around at CCTV you'll start to realize that a lot of systems have been installed without considering an attacker's mindset.

EXERCISE 7.1 Spot the security flaw

Given your newfound understanding of security issues around physical security, here is a 'spot the security flaw' list you can tick off whilst travelling around.

- CCTV camera positioned where an attacker could reach, move or unplug it.
- CCTV camera not covering what it should.
- Someone wearing their security badge or lanyard away from their office.
- Someone working in public where you can read their screen.
- Magnetic lock mounted on the unrestricted side (so it could be disabled).
- Someone tailgating access into an area covered by access control (eg into an office).

Physical vulnerabilities in the Internet of Things

The physical dimensions of cyber security have accelerated in recent years with the increasing connectivity of society. As highlighted by the Mirai botnet covered in Chapter 4 in relation to the Dyn DDoS (page 82), the expanding Internet of Things (IoT) means that more and more devices in our physical world are subject to cyber security vulnerabilities. In recent years we have seen internet-enabled watches, fitness trackers, spectacles, fridges, kettles, smart speakers, toothbrushes, thermostats, light bulbs, locks, doorbells, children's toys, sex toys and medical devices such as pacemakers. Security issues have been discovered with many of these devices, and the physical dimension of these can be disturbing.

In December 2019, an 8-year-old girl was in her bedroom when a criminal hacker spoke to her for ten minutes through a

Ring camera that had been installed so her mother could keep an eye on her daughter for medical reasons. The digital intruder told the girl he was Santa Claus, said that they were best friends and instructed her to call her mother terms of racist abuse. Upon investigating the incident, Ring found that it was the result of credential stuffing (covered in Chapter 4), in which criminals use passwords that have been breached in the past, to access other accounts that people have, relying on their re-use of passwords. There have been multiple reports of other people having their Ring cameras compromised in the same way.[2]

Vulnerabilities have been found in children's toys and watches, too: for example, in 2018 the security company Pen Test Partners found that they could track children's movements, covertly listen in to their activities and make spoof phone calls to a watch that looked like they were coming from the children's parents.[3] Of course, the risk that this could pose to children's physical security is very troubling.

The idea of 'smart cities' is no longer something from a science fiction movie, but rather a reality in which most of us are living, at least to some extent. Many of the systems that make up our cities, such as traffic light systems, advertising billboards, traffic signs and telephone networks, are now connected; they are therefore potentially vulnerable to being hacked. In 2017, all 156 warning sirens in the US city of Dallas (which are generally used to warn of extreme weather events) were hacked and activated in the middle of the night for approximately 90 minutes. In 2018, citizens of Hawaii received warning of an imminent missile attack via an emergency message sent to mobile phones. It took over half an hour for a follow-up message to be sent, stating that the warning had been sent in error and was a false alarm; apparently someone had pressed the wrong button and sent the emergency message by mistake.

THE PHYSICAL INFRASTRUCTURE OF THE INTERNET

The internet is not just a digital medium, of course. It has to live somewhere, and that somewhere is in dedicated computer systems called servers. These servers are often found in large buildings called data centres, and in order to talk to one another servers need to be connected to one another, either via cables made of copper or glass fibre optics that utilize laser beams to send data at the speed of light. Multiple devices are used to control the flow of data in and out of a data centre, such as network switches, firewalls, routers and more. All of the devices that play a role in getting data from a webserver in Google to your router at home need security in place. The large data centres of Google and Amazon or even your bank hold incalculable amounts of data and an attacker gaining physical access to any part of this infrastructure could potentially cause chaos or steal information.

Countries need to be connected together, too, otherwise companies in the US wouldn't be able to communicate with clients in the UK, for example. Large undersea cables are used to transmit vast swathes of data around the world and whilst the undersea portion is relatively difficult to gain access to, the landfall sections of these cables (where they come out of the sea and onto the land) must be heavily guarded against attack. There are currently just over 40 landfall sites around Great Britain alone, connecting us with other countries.

CASE STUDY   Colonial Pipeline

In May 2021, the largest pipeline for oil production in the United States had to shut down. A ransomware attack on the business systems at Colonial Pipeline put the company in a position where they had to shut the pipeline itself for days. This led to a spike in gasoline prices, panic buying and localized fuel shortages. It also prompted deeper questions about the relationship between digital and physical security and supply chains.

Colonial Pipeline were compromised via a virtual private network (VPN) that was protected only by a password, with no multi-factor authentication in place. Colonial Pipeline paid the ransom, reported to be $4.4 million after negotiations with the cyber criminals (some of which was later recovered by the FBI). The group apparently responsible for the attack, DarkSide, seemed to apologize for the disruption caused and stated that their intentions were only ever to make money and not cause social problems or engage in geopolitical matters.[4]

CASE STUDY   Florida water supply

You're not touching your computer mouse, but you see the cursor move around your screen all by itself. That would be pretty scary. It would be even more scary if you worked at a water supply plant and you saw the cursor access the treatment software and increase the sodium hydroxide content from 100 parts per million to 11,100 ppm. Thankfully, this would not have been enough to cause fatalities, but it could have caused harm and certainly highlights the potential for greater harm.

It sounds like the plot of a movie, but this is what happened at Florida Water Supply in February 2021. The plant operator who saw this unfold immediately set the chemical levels back to normal and the remote access system was disabled.

In Chapter 10, we will look at Stuxnet, the first cyber weapon that had a physical impact. Since then, there have been other examples of cyber attacks and incidents that have had physical ramifications. In 2017, a German steel mill was hacked and reportedly suffered massive damage when a blast furnace was compromised and could not be shut down. Attackers had apparently compromised the network of the steel mill by using spear-phishing emails to steal internal credentials that provided them access to the mill's control systems. In 2018, a petrochemical plant in Saudi Arabia was hacked, in what many suspect was a nation-state-sponsored attack, with the reported intention of causing an explosion (the attack failed due to a code error).

The physical dimensions of cyber security, therefore, can range from how a building is physically secured to ensure that its assets and information are protected, through to the physical infrastructure of our economies, industries, societies – and the internet itself. Cyber security is not just about protecting information and livelihoods – it is sometimes about protecting people's lives.

Notes

1 Warrell, H and Wright, R (2019) Balfour Beatty sacked from MI6 refurbishment contract, *Financial Times*, 27 December, www.ft.com/content/81d4ac8c-28d9-11ea-9a4f-963f0ec7e134 (archived at https://perma.cc/234D-3JJT)

2 Ritschel, C (2019) Mother releases video of hacker talking to eight-year-old child through Ring camera, *Independent*, 12 December, www.independent.co.uk/news/world/americas/ring-camera-video-hack-security-mississippi-child-a9244326.html (archived at https://perma.cc/64Z5-QJ62)

3 Kellon, L (2018) MiSafes' child-tracking smartwatches are 'easy to hack', BBC News, 15 November, www.bbc.co.uk/news/technology-46195189 (archived at https://perma.cc/PN89-X9U5)

4 https://www.vice.com/en/article/bvzzez/colonial-pipeline-hackers-statement-darkside (archived at https://perma.cc/8VJK-DEV5)

CHAPTER EIGHT

How organizations can better protect themselves

There is no one security solution that will protect an organization. As we have seen, security relies on a layered set of defences in conjunction with monitoring and testing of those defences to ensure that they maintain required levels of defence, detection and response. The first step in establishing a security programme is understanding the information assets you have and what value they represent for the organization, its clients or customers, and those who might seek to access and abuse the information. Cataloguing the assets and performing risk assessments is a fundamental part of establishing what level of security to ascribe to which systems and assets, and therefore which controls to put in place. Using a framework (such as the National Institute of Standards and Technology (NIST) Cybersecurity Framework or ISO 27001) will help many organizations with the process of categorizing information assets, conducting risk assessments and determining appropriate controls (as we will discuss in Chapter 12).

In this chapter, we are going to look at the common security controls and practices that organizations use to better protect themselves.

Firewalls

Firewalls are commonly regarded as the first line of defence in cyber security, a gateway that is intended to protect an internal, secured network from threats that exist on the open internet. A firewall sits on the network, as hardware and/or software, and monitors traffic that is coming in and going out. Using a set of rules, it determines traffic that is authorized or expected to come into the network and where it can go. The rules revolve around the data source, destination and ports. A simple analogy would be to imagine a security desk in a shared building as the firewall; the security desk decides who can be allowed in and where they are able to go within the building, depending on who they are and how trusted they are.

Anti-virus software

Anti-virus software can also be understood as anti-malware. It traditionally works by detecting and removing computer viruses and malicious software, running in the background of systems and searching for signatures of known malware (if you imagine that each piece of malware has a fingerprint, it is searching for the fingerprint). A key limitation of this, of course, is that it can only detect and remove known malware; it uses a database of known malware signatures and so, when a new threat emerges, its signature will not be in the database. Due to this limitation, anti-virus protections have evolved to monitor the system and pick up on unusual behaviour: when the system does something that is unusual, the anti-virus is triggered. Advances in machine learning have been incorporated in anti-virus, enabling the systems to learn from new data, behaviours and signatures.

Network segmentation

Network segmentation is a very important element in an organization's defences, based on the understanding that organizations must not only try to protect against being attacked, but also put in place damage limitation for if (or when) they are breached. Network segmentation means that if one part of an organization or its network is compromised, this compromise can be contained and not infect the whole. This also allows for logical segmentation of an organization, so that different departments have different segments. It works in conjunction with what is called the 'least privilege' principle – that users can only access the minimum that they need in order to do their work – meaning that access to information can be structured more easily on a need to know basis. It also allows for better monitoring and auditing of access to information. This is superior to a flat network, in which nothing is segmented and people can move around the network more freely, accessing information that perhaps should not be available to them.

AIRGAPPED NETWORKS

When a segmented network is not enough and more control is required over a system or some particular information, organizations will build an airgapped network, meaning a network that does not touch the internet or any other part of the existing network. An airgapped network is a standalone, solitary system that is built to resist infection from outside. Airgapped systems are used in the military, defence firms and industrial control systems. As covered in Chapter 11, reports suggest that an airgapped

---

computer was used successfully by *Vanity Fair* magazine in 2015 to protect their global exclusive covering Caitlyn Jenner's transformation.[1] As covered in Chapter 10, the Stuxnet attack compromised an airgapped system at the Natanz facility, spread by an infected USB stick, confirming that of course airgapped systems are – like anything – not 100 per cent secure.

Policies and procedures

Organizations use policies and procedures to capture and communicate expectations, responsibilities and commitments regarding cyber security. They may not be exciting, but they are important as a way of ensuring that the organization has communicated what is expected of people – for example, acceptable use of the internet, password management, what to do if there has been an incident, and who is responsible for cyber security. Some policies are legally required or required for compliance purposes, and they should also be in place to provide legal protection for employees and for the organization. Unfortunately, policies are often neglected or ignored. In 2019, research from ClubCISO found that 53 per cent of senior information security leaders who took part in the survey stated that they believed their policies are ineffective, dormant or don't affect day-to-day behaviours.[2] For policies to be effective and useful, it is important they are kept up to date, that they are written in jargon-free and concise language, that people know where to find them in the organization (for example, that they are easy to navigate to on the intranet) and that relevant information is easy to find within them.

Logging

Logging is the recording of events that relate to the security of systems. The information that is logged depends on the requirements, but examples include what information has been accessed, when, and by which user account. Logs should be auditable and audited. One mistake organizations often make with logs is collecting too much information, making them unwieldy and drowning out the useful information. It is important that logs are regularly reviewed, not just in terms of auditing events that have occurred but also considering whether the information being collected is still of value.

Monitoring

Monitoring is usually carried out in the background of systems, aiming to detect attacks and ensure that systems are being used according to organizational policies. Monitoring enables organizations to detect attacks; the quicker an organization can identify an attack, the better positioned it is to respond. Monitoring is also often required as part of legal and regulatory requirements. As with logging, organizations can fall foul of attempting to monitor too much, which can lead to false positives and the danger of becoming desensitized to alerts, which can lead to true incidents being overlooked.

Auditing

Security audits are a review of an organization's cyber security policies, systems and controls, and they can be performed both internally and externally. A security audit can include vulnerability scans and penetration tests (see below), cultural assessments (see below), reviewing access controls, assessing physical security and more. Audits are often a regulatory requirement and can be part of an organization meeting a security standard, such as ISO 27001. Audits can be regarded as a 'tick box exercise', conducted simply for the sake of compliance, but when conducted as part of a genuine drive to assess and improve security they can provide valuable and actionable insights.

Intrusion detection systems and intrusion protection systems

An intrusion detection system (IDS) is used to observe network traffic and identify intrusions, looking for malicious activity or policy violations. An IDS usually works in conjunction with security information and event management (SIEM) systems, with the IDS reporting information to the SIEM and the SIEM alerting on malicious activity and filtering out false alarms. Problems occur with these systems when there are errors, and systems that fail to identify intrusions, or that provide too few or too many alerts (either not reporting intrusions or reporting too many false flags).

Intrusion protection systems (IPS) go one step further than IDS; when an IPS identifies a suspected intrusion attempt, it will act upon it; for example, blocking the IP address from where an identified attack is coming.

Block list and allow list

Block lists and allow lists are used to determine what is either approved or denied, by default, in terms of access. They can be applied to all sorts of commodities including domains, software, IP addresses and passwords. Allow lists are when organizations set the sites and software (for example) that people are allowed to use, with everything else blocked, and block lists are when access to everything is open apart from the websites and software that are captured on the list. There is usually then a process that people can go through to request that a website or piece of software is made available to them if they make a business case for it; for example, social media sites may be blocked, but a marketing team would need access to them and so they have an exemption for valid business reasons. As with so many areas, striking a balance between security and usability is important, because being too restrictive can hamper people's ability to do their jobs and promote the perception that security is a blocker to the business. You may come across block and allow lists referred to as black lists and white lists – they mean the same thing, although there is a growing belief that these latter terms are outdated and inappropriate.

Cyber threat intelligence and threat hunting

Cyber threat intelligence is used in different ways, but in this context it means the activities that organizations undertake to research and analyse trends in terms of cyber attacks. For example, the Cyber Security Information Sharing Partnership (CiSP) in the UK is a joint industry and government initiative that facilitates the secure sharing of information on cyber threats in real time. Organizations that are approved as members of CiSP use the platform, and other threat intelligence feeds, to stay up to date on information about the latest cyber security issues.

Threat hunting is an active defence activity within the area of cyber threat intelligence. Threat hunting involves proactively searching for, detecting, isolating and managing threats. Threat hunters work within the network, with the perspective that attackers have already compromised the system, and use tools combined with their expertise to identify suspicious activity. As well as a strong level of technical expertise, threat hunters require professional skills including communication and team-working abilities, to be able to share their findings in an actionable way.

Vulnerability scanning

Vulnerability scans are automated assessments of a network, with the purpose of identifying known vulnerabilities in firewalls, applications and other devices. Even small organizations will usually have the ability to conduct vulnerability scans on a fairly regular basis due to the automation available either using software themselves or using a third-party provider such as a penetration testing company. It is important that vulnerability scanning is not confused with penetration testing, though – a vulnerability scan will only find known vulnerabilities, and will not be nuanced enough to address issues of impact and business implications.

Penetration testing

Taking vulnerability scanning to another level and beyond is penetration testing, or pen testing (also called ethical hacking). Pen testing involves assessing computer systems and software to find security vulnerabilities and how these vulnerabilities could be exploited, within a defined scope that is usually set by the organization. It is a common regulatory requirement. Pen testers will often use the operating system Kali Linux, which includes tools such as Burp Suite, Metasploit and OpenVAS; the tools will support the professional in doing their work, but they do not do the assessment for them. Pen testing requires the technical skills to identify vulnerabilities and – depending on the terms of the engagement – to either exploit the vulnerabilities, or to understand how they could be exploited. Pen testing also requires the professional expertise to recognize the potential impact of these issues and communicate the findings in a way that makes sense to both the technical team and the senior executives.

Awareness-raising training

Awareness-raising training comes in many forms, and there are many innovative approaches that are in a different league to some of the dry and ineffective approaches of the past (how many people have clicked through a dull computer-based training module or snoozed their way through a boring presentation without learning a thing?). In my experience, the most effective training is tailored to the recipient, engaging and experiential; for example, live hacking demonstrations are often really powerful. It's important to use case studies that are relevant to the audience, clearly communicate without unnecessary jargon, create an environment where people are comfortable asking questions and discuss cyber security not just in terms of the workplace, but in relation to people's personal lives as well.

There are so many things that we need people to be aware of, from social engineering threats to good security practices, including password management, multi-factor authentication and how they use social media (how individuals can better protect themselves is covered in detail in Chapter 9). However, the aim of awareness-raising training is not just to change people's behaviours in terms of specific threats, because the threats can change, but rather to positively influence their security mindset and enhance their situational awareness. Entertaining people, at the same time as educating and informing them, helps keep people engaged and interested, and means they are more likely to go away from the awareness-raising talking positively about it and spreading the messages.

Security culture

More and more organizations are recognizing that the most effective awareness-raising training will be in harmony with organizational culture. When considering what culture is, I find a definition provided by MIT Professor Edgar Schien to be very helpful: he explains organizational culture as the *values and beliefs* that underpin the *norms of expected behaviours* that employees may follow.[3]

Organizational culture is very influential on security; it can influence everything from whether people write their passwords on a piece of paper and stick it to their desks, to how likely someone is to report an incident and whether the developers will work with the security team from the outset of building a new product. When I am helping organizations consider their cyber security awareness, behaviour and culture programmes, I will encourage them to firstly consider what kind of organizational culture they have, and what kind of cyber security culture they want. This often involves cultural assessments and analysis to make sure that we truly understand what the company culture is like and how (and why) it differs from team to team and at different levels. From that, we will look at the behaviours that would exemplify the kind of cyber security culture that they are looking to engender. The final piece of the puzzle is awareness: what awareness-raising initiatives would fit with the wider company culture whilst positively influencing behavioural change?

Champion programmes

They can go by many names, but security champion programmes are when people throughout the organization represent security; they are not security professionals and they are not expected to be experts, but instead they function in a similar way to fire wardens or health and safety representatives. They may get some additional training, and have access to resources and a source of expertise if they need it. Their role is usually to push out security messages to their team, listen to people in their part of the organization with regards to security (what communications are being understood, what security worries do people have, what would they like to know more about) and often be the first port of call if someone has a worry, such as thinking they may have clicked on a link in a phishing email. Champion programmes are a great way of scaling up security, of listening to the organization and providing a friendly, known face for security throughout different teams. The champions can provide social proof, showing that security is relevant in different teams and leading the way for positive behaviours. Champion programmes are not one-size-fits-all; they can take some designing to make sure that the logistics have been considered at the outset and, like all of the measures in this chapter, they certainly aren't a silver bullet, but they can be hugely effective as part of a positive security programme.

Digital footprint assessments

Targeted social engineering attacks often utilize information that attackers have gathered from social media. This is not to say that people should not use social media, of course – it can have lots of personal and professional benefits – but it does mean that many organizations seek to educate people within the business about how information they have shared, or that is shared about them online, can be used in social engineering attempts. Some organizations do this by undertaking digital footprint assessments (sometimes called open source intelligence, or OSINT, assessments) to determine the information that is online about high-risk individuals or groups within the organization (for example, senior executives and their personal assistants). This can be categorized as part of an organization's cyber intelligence activities. The results of these assessments will often be used to raise awareness with the targets about the extent of their digital footprint online and how the information could be used in social engineering attacks. Of course, these assessments (like all security measures) must be conducted according to legal and ethical considerations.

Physical security controls

As covered in Chapter 7, physical security is a core pillar of cyber security. That chapter explored some of the most fundamental physical security measures, but one physical security control we haven't properly looked at yet is locks. Locks are considered the most basic of physical security controls, and they have evolved from traditional locks with keys, to combination locks that use codes, to 'smart locks' that use computer-based access control measures (as well as magnetic locks, which were covered in Chapter 7). All locks can be circumvented, of course, which doesn't mean they do not have a place in security; it just means that they should be considered as only one layer of defence and not a solution in and of themselves.

Social engineering assessments and red team engagements

I am using social engineering assessments here in its widest sense, to include physical assessments. The premise of these is that an organization's security is tested in terms of whether someone can 'break in' either by socially engineering members of staff or by circumventing physical security controls. Red team assessments take this a step further; they are an amalgamation of social engineering, physical attacks and penetration testing. Some very large organizations will have their own internal red team while others will use external companies, and they will usually pen test the digital network as well as perform physical and social engineering attacks to test the security of the organization from different angles. The red team is often given little to no scope restrictions and can be given almost carte blanche to affect an organization within the limits of legal and ethical guidelines.

One issue with these assessments is that they are highly likely to always be successful, because it is impossible for an organization to be 100 per cent secure. This can give the perception that security is failing, and it can lead to a skewed perspective over which security measures should be prioritized. For these reasons, I would argue that these assessments are best suited to organizations that already have a high level of security maturity and who want to test a particular control (such as a newly installed door or a procedure for welcoming visitors to the office) or who want to use the results as part of awareness-raising activities.

A layered approach

This chapter has covered some of the most important security controls that organizations can put in place to better protect themselves. Of course, to cover everything would take a whole book in itself, and entire books can be (and are!) written on each topic in isolation. One of the most important messages to understand is that there is no one security solution, but rather a layered approach – which does not just try to defend an organization, but also recognizes that we need to be prepared for when a breach happens – offers the best defence. One of the most important, and complicated, layers of defence is human behaviour. In the next chapter, we will look at what people can do to better protect themselves, which not only has individual benefits but also organizational, economic and societal benefits.

Notes

1   Miller, J (2015) The inside story of Caitlyn Jenner's historic *Vanity Fair* cover, *Vanity Fair*, 27 July, www.vanityfair.com/hollywood/2015/07/caitlyn-jenner-documentary (archived at https://perma.cc/LFX8-B4AZ)

2   ClubCISO (2019) Information security maturity report 2019: Full survey results, www.clubciso.org/downloads/ (archived at https://perma.cc/L4XX-VX2Y)

3   Schein, EH (1992) *Organizational Culture and Leadership*, Jossey-Bass Inc, San Francisco.

CHAPTER NINE

How individuals can better protect themselves

In an ideal world, digital technology would be secure by default and people would be able to use the internet and smart devices intuitively and safely, without having to undertake extra steps to keep their information and, often, their finances safe. Unfortunately, we do not live in an ideal world, and the internet has not been built to be secure by default. Cyber security professionals often make the mistake of overwhelming people with information. We should not expect everyone to become a security or technology expert to be able to use the internet and enjoy the benefits of connected technology. We do not need everyone to understand all of the esoteric, atypical elements of cyber security, and we do not make anyone more secure when we inflate our sense of self-importance by telling people that the internet is broken. We shouldn't expect people to run before they are walking. Instead of telling people the 100 ways they or their company could be affected by cyber insecurity – and the 200 things they need to do to protect against that – let's start with the core behaviours they can put in place to better protect themselves, and keep building on that. It is important to help people with these core behaviours in the same way that we learn how to drive a car safely; we don't expect everyone to understand the intricacies of how an engine works, but we are all expected to drive a car without endangering ourselves and others.

Protect your accounts

There are so many case studies in this book that highlight the security issues of weak passwords and poor password management. Passwords are the key to our online accounts; if we use weak passwords, or we re-use passwords, we open the potential for our accounts to be easily compromised by dictionary attacks or credential stuffing (as covered elsewhere in this book, for example Chapters 3 and 4). People use weak passwords, and re-use them across their accounts, because they have a large number of accounts, they struggle to remember unique, complicated passwords and they do not think they would be a target of cybercrime (misunderstanding the nature of cybercrime, falsely believing that they would have to be individually targeted for their accounts to be compromised). The first step in encouraging people to approach their passwords more securely, therefore, is helping people understand that this is something we all need to do, that their accounts can be compromised without a hacker singling them out and targeting them directly.

In recent years, there has been a move away from passwords and towards passphrases or three random words. The idea behind this advice is that longer, more complicated passwords offer more security and so, if people can use phrases or sets of words, those should be more memorable and, in theory, more secure. Some security experts dispute the efficacy of passphrases and three random words. Looking at the recommendation from a usability perspective, a pressing issue with the advice is that it is not scalable: people may be able to remember one good passphrase or set of random words, but can they remember enough to use across all of their different accounts? Bear in mind that research suggests people have as many as 90, or more, online accounts.

Re-use is arguably the most pressing security issue when it comes to passwords. To overcome the security issues with password re-use I recommend individuals either use a password manager or – I hope you're sitting down for this – write their passwords down. The latter sounds like classic terrible security advice, doesn't it? Well, hear me out: there are good reasons for the advice and, most importantly, some crucial caveats. Before we get to that, let's look at password managers.

Password managers

Password managers are what their name implies, they are tools to generate, store and manage passwords, acting like a vault. There are different options available, from ones that you run on your computer to cloud-based password managers that enable you to access your passwords on your different devices. You generally need to access the password manager with a password, so it is important that this password is a very secure one (by which I mean long and complicated), but this should be the only password you need to remember. The benefits of password managers are many:

- They take away the mental burden of having to think up secure passwords.
- They take away the mental burden of having to remember many secure passwords.
- Many will automatically log you in to accounts.
- If you need to share passwords, for example with your spouse or colleagues, many will provide a secure way for you to do that.

- Most are free for personal use (password managers are generally based on a business model that charges organizations a fee, but not individuals).

I just mentioned another password no-no, didn't I? Sharing passwords. It is common security advice that people should never share passwords and, like most sweeping security advice, it is unrealistic and unhelpful. There are many times where we need to share passwords, from the family account for a TV streaming service to a corporate social media account, to the harsh reality of enabling access to household accounts if the main account holder dies. If we continue to give security advice that is not aligned with reality, we will continue to be ignored. Instead, let's understand how people live and work, and provide advice that takes that into account.

For me, this is the beauty of password managers. Password managers recognize that the cognitive burden of creating and remembering unique passwords for a number of online accounts is too great for the vast majority of people. This cognitive burden is why people will create a Word, Excel or Notes document on their computers to save all of their passwords in. This is not a secure way of storing passwords; if the device is compromised, one of the first things a cyber criminal will do is look for such a file. So, password managers are the secure version of that. People often ask how secure it really is to put all of your eggs in one basket, to entrust all of your passwords to a password manager. This is a great, and valid, question. The way I see it is that password managers are much more secure than what most people are doing now, which is re-using weak passwords. Password management companies put way more time, effort, expertise and money into securing their product than I can put into managing my passwords myself. If they become compromised, their business is over, which is quite an incentive for ensuring that they maintain as good a level of security as possible.

If we, as security professionals, cannot follow our own advice, then we need to accept that the advice is wrong. If it is too unrealistic for those of us who spend our days focused on security, it is definitely too unrealistic for everyone else.

Writing passwords down

The drive for realistic security advice is why I sometimes recommend that people write their passwords down. Although a password manager would always be my preferred recommendation, it is not the perfect solution for everyone. They can be a bit complicated to set up and use, which will be off-putting for people. In instances where someone does not want to use a password manager, or cannot use a password manager, it is far better for people to write down their passwords in a dedicated notebook, than it is for them to re-use weak passwords. If people are not using a password manager or writing their passwords down, it is overwhelmingly likely that they are re-using weak passwords.

Security is ultimately about threat models, by which I mean identifying potential threats, understanding them and putting in place mitigations where possible. When thinking about having a password notebook, consider your threat model. What are the potential threats to a notebook full of your usernames and passwords? If you take it out of the house with you, it could be lost or stolen, so I would recommend keeping it at home where possible and, if you do take it out of your home, treat it like your wallet. When keeping it at home, recognize that anyone you share your home with may find the book and use the passwords to get into your accounts. If that poses a threat to you or would be a problem to you, then a password notebook may not be suitable for your threat model. Or, you might still want to consider a password notebook but with some extra mitigations in place, such as locking it in a safe and using a code that you can remember for your credentials (eg changing every letter that is upper case in your passwords to lower case ones when you write them down, writing down your passwords backwards or using something like the Caeser shift). Bear in mind that codes can be broken and, again, your threat model will determine how much you want to mitigate against this with a complicated code.

What are the other potential threats to keeping a password notebook at home? It is far more likely that someone will break into weak, recycled passwords over the internet than that they will break into your home and steal your book of passwords as a way of compromising your internet accounts. A password notebook is not something I would recommend people use in an office, not least because it will probably be a policy violation, but for many people it will offer them stronger, and more manageable, cyber security at home.

BIOMETRIC SECURITY

In 2004, Bill Gates spoke at the RSA conference in San Francisco and stated that the use of passwords would soon die. Over fifteen years later, and passwords are still very much with us. However, in recent years, we have seen an increase in the use of biometric systems, as discussed in Chapter 7. Home technology users are embracing biometric authentication for devices such as their smart phones and, although there have been many examples of biometric authentication being compromised, these systems may be a better approach to security than passwords or PINs. For example, it would be more secure for an individual to use fingerprint scanning or facial recognition to access their device than to use a simple PIN such as 0000 or a common pin such as a date, like 1976. If their phone is pickpocketed, it would take a more sophisticated criminal to lift and clone their fingerprint, than it would to brute force their PIN (or shoulder surf it before they steal the phone).

Two-factor authentication

Passwords should not be the only layer of security on your online accounts; two-factor authentication is vital, so that if your password is compromised or not kept safe by the account provider, your accounts are as secure as possible. We looked at what two-factor authentication (2FA) is, why it is important and the different options in Chapter 4. One issue I did not address there is the lack of take-up of 2FA; in 2019, I surveyed 1,000 people in the UK and found that only 26 per cent of those were using 2FA where possible, and 62 per cent did not know what it was.[1]

We need to find a way to encourage more uptake of 2FA. Providers are reluctant to make 2FA use default for their services, as they don't want to force it on people and lose customers. However, some companies are taking an innovative approach to encourage engagement with 2FA. The games company EA ran a campaign in which they gave away a free month of the game Origin Access to players who had 2FA enabled or who activated it. EA were following in the footsteps of the marketing platform Mailchimp, which provides a 10 per cent discount for three months when customers enable 2FA. Research suggests that when these incentives are well chosen, they can lead to greater adoption of 2FA.[2]

LOYALTY POINTS THEFT

Cyber criminals follow the money, and are always looking for new ways to make a profit. So, whilst we may not think much about the loyalty card schemes we sign up to, there are signs that loyalty card point theft is on the rise. The crime is, quite simply, when criminals target our loyalty card points and steal them – and it could be carried out in a number of ways, one of the most likely being account compromise via credential stuffing. If someone is re-using an email address and password that has been breached elsewhere, or indeed if they are simply using a weak password, that is a likely way for cyber criminals to access their account and steal their points.

Another way that criminals carry out fraud such as loyalty point theft is via card cloning. Using a card skimmer device, which a fraudster can use to swipe your card and steal the details from it, criminals are able to build cloned cards using your details (this can be used for everything from loyalty cards to credit cards). Card cloning is why it is important to never hand your cards over to someone, even someone working in a store or coffee shop, but instead to always swipe it yourself.

Loyalty point theft can also be carried out by criminals using malware, spread for example via malicious apps (discussed below) or phishing emails and messages, which could also be used to steal your username and password. This highlights an important point. It may seem that cyber criminals are always coming up with new and different ways to defraud us, which seems overwhelming, but the vast majority of these new frauds are based on known and established methods such as phishing and credential stuffing. If we follow the advice contained in this chapter to better protect ourselves, we are putting in place mitigations that will protect us from most cybercrime in operation no matter how 'new' it may seem.

Protect your devices

A key message we need to communicate to people, to help them stay more secure, is the importance of keeping their devices and apps up to date. We have taught people to ignore pop-ups on their computers, which is good when it comes to pop-ups themselves but bad when it comes to something that appears similar to a pop-up: automatically generated update prompts. On top of this issue, people are busy and security updates often seem to appear when people don't feel they have the time to do them (this is because security is rarely the primary reason for using a laptop, tablet or phone, so whenever the update prompt arrives, people will be engaged in something else).

In Chapter 3, we looked at the prevalence of vulnerabilities and the work that goes into identifying and fixing these. When a vulnerability is identified and patched, that patch must be applied everywhere the software is in use, or the vulnerability will be exploitable. When the vulnerability becomes public knowledge, patching is even more important (the more people who know about the vulnerability, the more chance there is that people are attempting to exploit it). This is why timely updates are important. Let's say I am using a banking application and a vulnerability is discovered in it; for example, allowing other users to access my account. A patch is developed for the vulnerability and an update is pushed out to all, to encourage everyone to apply the patch. If I, as an end-user, do not follow the update prompt, then my account still has the vulnerability and a criminal could exploit it. By keeping devices, software and apps updated, I am ensuring they are as secure as possible.

It is also important to be careful with the apps we download on our phones and tablets, checking they are reputable and trusted apps before we install them. This is because criminals use apps to spread malware, enabling them to steal data including usernames, passwords, financial data and personal information. The iPhone app store scrutinizes apps more rigorously than Android, so be especially careful if you use an Android device (but don't believe that you are immune just because you are using an Apple device).

As well as keeping devices updated, we also need to consider the physical security of them. Smart phones are small computers that many of us carry around with us, and access to the phone usually comes with access to lots of apps that are generally automatically logged in. This can include our emails, social media accounts and shopping sites with stored financial data. This is why using a screen lock on your phone is really important, as is making sure that lock isn't too simple (for example, don't use

1234 as a PIN or a 'U' shape for pattern unlock). I also recommend that individuals enable settings that allow them to remotely wipe their devices, so if your phone is stolen you can remove all data from it.

Protect your data

On websites

The green padlock that often shows in the URL bar when you visit a website is meant to show that the website is secure. In reality, it does not mean that the website is secure; if only security was that simple. The padlock means that the website is using a Secure Sockets Layer (SSL) certificate, which means that it is running https not http. This means that your connection to the website is encrypted. Whilst it is recommended to use websites that are encrypted, especially if you are sharing personal data, the fact that the site you are on is encrypted does not by default make it a secure one. Cyber criminals have found ways to fake security certificates or obtain them with false details and so there are malicious sites that display the padlock sign, seeking to lull people into a false sense of security. A padlock is just one sign of whether a site is authentic and to be trusted.

Criminals use fake websites for all sorts of things. Sometimes fake websites are used to sell counterfeit goods, sometimes they are used to steal people's personal and financial data; sometimes they are used for both. When we buy goods online, we provide a lot of personal and financial data and this opens the potential for the criminals running scam sites to steal this data. Criminals do different things with stolen data: they may sell it to other criminals, they may carry out fraud on us directly by accessing our bank accounts, or they may use our data to set up scam sites in our names and with our details.

Spotting a scam website is about looking at the site as a whole and identifying any anomalies, such as spelling and grammatical errors, poor photographs and links to other content that fail to load. You can check reviews of the website and also see where it is based; for example, if there is a UK, European or US postal address.

Backing up

The rise of ransomware, as discussed in Chapter 1, has affected individuals and home users as well as organizations. Many people now store a great deal of data digitally, which can include sentimental items such as family photographs. To prevent losing these in a ransomware attack or computer failure, it is recommended that individuals regularly back up their data, for example using external hard drives. Just be sure to disconnect it and store it safely when you are not actively using it.

Be social media savvy

Without a password manager or password notebook, people are likely to use passwords that are memorable to them, such as names of family members, favourite football teams, pets' names and favourite musicians. This is problematic because these are generally common, so are likely to be included in dictionary attacks on passwords, but also because it is information that many of us also share on social media.

Cyber criminals use information we share on social media not just to compromise passwords but also to craft more successful social engineering attacks. This is not to say we should not enjoy the benefits of social media, but rather that we should have an awareness of the way it can be used maliciously. Reviewing our privacy and security settings enables us to make sure that information is as private as we wish it to be. Ensuring that we use a strong, unique password and have 2FA set up mitigates our account being compromised. In protecting our social media accounts, we also protect those we are connected to, as compromised accounts are often used by criminals to spread spam and links to scam sites. With this in mind, we should be aware that we can't always trust the links that our contacts share on social media and, as the example of 'Janessa Brazil' showed us in Chapter 6, people are not always who they seem to be online.

Be social engineering savvy

The 'Janessa Brazil' example shows us that social engineering comes in many forms; it is not just about phishing emails. It is important that people understand that any way in which someone communicates with us can be abused by social engineering, whether this is email, social media, messaging platforms, phone calls, letters or people turning up in person on our doorsteps.

In August 2019, news outlets warned people of a new mobile phone scam, which involved social engineering carried out face-to-face combined with digital fraud. The scam works like this: a package is delivered to your door, with your name on, containing a new smart phone. Not long afterwards, there is another knock at the door with another courier explaining they delivered it by mistake and ask for the phone back. This delivery scam is based on identity theft: the criminals have used your details to order a phone (or other high-value item), which they then try to intercept at delivery. They are making a purchase using your (stolen) details and then taking that purchase from you, which they will sell, leaving you to pay for it in the first place.

This scam highlights the importance of awareness, not just of the latest scams but also the underlying methods and criminal mindset at play. Cyber criminals will always find new tactics to carry out their activities, but these are rooted in the same general techniques and strategies. Following the steps covered in this chapter will protect individuals against most cybercrime in operation:

1 Protect your accounts with strong, unique passwords and 2FA.
2 Be aware of card cloning, and don't let other people handle your cards, especially to take to a device that you cannot see.
3 Protect your devices by keeping them up to date and taking care with the apps you download.
4 Protect your data on public Wi-Fi by avoiding doing anything sensitive (such as online banking) and consider using a trusted VPN.
5 Be aware of the websites you use, particularly if you are buying something or inputting your personal or financial data.
6 Be social media savvy, with an awareness of the information you share and the fact that people are not always who they appear to be online.
7 It's not just online that people are not always who they appear to be; social engineering crosses the digital, physical and social world and is used in all sorts of crimes.

Underpinning all of these tips is awareness. Knowing that these crimes are carried out, how the criminals are doing it and what we can do to better protect ourselves is the first step.

The right phish at the wrong time can catch us all. Traditionally, cyber security advice would often be to 'avoid clicking on suspicious links'. This puts too much burden on people without offering them much to work with. Spotting a suspicious link is not always so easy – especially as social engineering emails and messages get increasingly convincing. Other advice includes looking out for grammatical or spelling errors, checking the sender's address (by clicking on it to expand it and hovering over the link to see where it is pointing).

This advice can sometimes help us identify phishing – but certainly not always, which opens a danger that we lull ourselves into a false sense of security. Phishing messages don't always include errors (and the ones that do sometimes do on purpose, to focus on those most likely to ultimately be scammed). On some devices, it's difficult or impossible to expand the sender's address or hover over the link. And many phishing messages don't include malicious links. Many have malicious attachments or encourage the recipient to share information or transfer money. Others are designed to lure targets in, for example warming them up to social engineering that then follows over a phone call. Finally, you may look at the sender's address and feel reassured that an email comes from the legitimate, expected address, but this does not necessarily mean that the email itself is legitimate: what if the account has been compromised? To make matters worse, many legitimate emails look a bit phishy.

Cyber criminals evolve their tactics. When we just teach a tactical response to phishing, we don't build resilience and we fail to future-proof our defences. As well as technical layers of defence, at the individual level one of our best defences is our mindset. This is why I encourage you to tune into your emotional response to communications and be alert to anything that is unexpected, makes you feel something, and asks you to do something. Not every phish will prompt an emotional response, but the ones that make us feel worried, scared, curious, flattered or hurried are the ones more likely to be successful. They are the ones that cloud our judgement and push us into acting before we think. Being vigilant is the most valuable approach, a mindset that embraces situational awareness and trusts your instincts. Check with the supposed sender – via a channel you know you can trust – to see if they really did send you that message or make that call.

Notes

1   Barker, J (2019) 62% of people do not know what two-factor authentication is: Our survey of 1,000 people in the UK (blog), Cygenta, 4 October, https://blog. cygenta.co.uk/2fa_2019 (archived at https://perma.cc/84RK-7NSU)
2   Busse, K, et al (2019) 'Get a free item pack with every activation': Do incentives increase the adoption rates of two-factor authentication? *Journal of Interactive Media*, Special Issue on Usable Security and Privacy, https://arxiv.org/ abs/1910.07269 (archived at https://perma.cc/GZH8-CZME)

CHAPTER TEN

Nation-state cyber security: Geopolitics

As we have seen already from some of the examples in this book so far, there is an inherent tension in how we approach cyber security at a global level. The digital sphere doesn't have boundaries in the same way that states – and therefore legislation and legal jurisdiction – do.

Policing the internet

This is one reason why policing the internet is so difficult: crimes can be conducted in one country while targeting another, and even if the attackers are identified with any certainty, taking legal action can be challenging or impossible, because it relies on countries working in collaboration. To try to mitigate this, there are frameworks in place to facilitate and manage this collaboration as much as possible.

The Tallinn Manual 2.0

The *Tallinn Manual 2.0: International Law Applicable to Cyber Operations* (*Tallinn Manual*), the drafting of which was led by the NATO Cooperative Cyber Defence Centre of Excellence, is a comprehensive analysis of how existing international law applies to cyberspace. Some broad conclusions we can take from the *Tallinn Manual* include that sovereignty applies to cyberspace, that state jurisdiction should apply in regards to cyber activities, and that states are responsible for cyber acts that are attributable to them and comprise a breach of international law (including actions by non-state actors that are carried out under the effective control of the state).[1] Of course, the *Tallinn Manual* contains much more analysis of international law regarding cyber activity, and there are many points where the experts who contributed to it express disagreement. This is a new and expanding area of law, which is moving rapidly, as we will see from some of the case studies in this chapter.

The Wassenaar Arrangement

The Wassenaar Arrangement (Wassenaar) was established in 1996, taking its name from a suburb of The Hague, in the Netherlands, where international agreement was reached in 1995 to start the multilateral cooperation. The aim of the arrangement is to contribute to international stability by regulating global trade in weaponry. Forty-two countries currently participate in the arrangement on a voluntary basis, including the UK, US, Ukraine, the Russian Federation, Estonia, the Netherlands, Japan and Australia.

In 2013, Wassenaar was amended to include command and delivery platforms for 'intrusion software' and 'intrusion software technology', classifying both of these as items that would require export licences in the same way as physical weapons. In the cyber security community, this wording caused confusion and concern, because it would have required export control licences for those involved in defensive security activities. This posed the potential for serious unintended consequences, for example that the technical response to real-time attacks could be held up in the processing of export control paperwork.

In 2017, the reworking of Wassenaar was agreed, thanks to expert input from Katie Moussouris and Iain Mulholland, so that cross-border sharing of vulnerabilities disclosures and security incident response are exempt from the export control licences that Wassenaar covers.[2]

Wassenaar reflects some of the issues that we face when trying to manage cyber security at the national and international level, as rules and regulations that make sense in the physical domain do not necessarily translate to the cyber domain. This example highlights the importance of having people with cyber security expertise involved in the formulation of such international agreements, to understand and explain how regulations that might make sense in theory will actually play out in practice.

The International Traffic in Arms Regulations

Nothing shows that cyber-based exploits are being seen as comparable to kinetic weapons more than regulation. The International Traffic in Arms Regulations (ITAR) have been used by the US since 1976 to restrict and control the export of military technologies in order to protect the US from foreign powers looking to leverage their own weapons against them or their allies. It controls the export of the assets that appear on the United States Munitions List (USML). At the time of writing, the USML is separated into 21 categories, covering everything from firearms through to chemical agents and nuclear weapons. As software developed for tailored access will often fall under ITAR, it is clear that the US among other countries recognizes that so-called cyber weapons have the potential to be as valuable and as devastating as more traditional weaponry.

Nation-state-level cyber attacks

While nation-state-level cyber activity is something that hits the headlines more frequently now than ever before, it is of course not new. Nation-state-level cyber activity is an extension of more traditional kinetic nation-state activity, including traditional methods of warfare intended to destabilize and disrupt, as well as activities of the intelligence agencies. But it is also different. Cyber activity at the nation-state level can cause disruption, distrust and disharmony in an insidious way, staying below the radar of kinetic forms of warfare whilst still having a very real impact.

The Great Seal

Also known as 'The Thing', the Great Seal bug is often listed as the first covert listening device, bridging the gap between traditional spycraft and modern sophisticated espionage. The bug was allegedly concealed inside a gift given by the Soviet Union to the US Ambassador to Russia on 4 August 1945. It required no power and is considered to be the forerunner of radio-frequency identification (RFID) technology.

The bug was hidden inside a large wooden plaque, bearing the Great Seal of America, which was hung in the residency of the US Ambassador for seven years. The device itself worked only when it was energized by an external powerful beam of radio energy, which enabled it to then function as both a microphone, picking up the room's audio, and as a transmitter to a nearby Russian listening station. The discovery of the bug was made by accident when a British radio operator heard the Americans having a conversation on an open channel.[3]

The Bronze Statue

In 2007, a dispute over a statue of a soldier led to Estonia becoming the victim of a disinformation campaign and a series of cyber attacks in what is widely regarded as the first act of cyber warfare in the world.[4] In 1947, the Bronze Soldier statue was unveiled by Soviet authorities in the centre of Tallinn, the nation's capital. The statue was divisive: embraced by the Russian-speaking population of Estonia as a symbol of liberation, but rejected by the indigenous population as a symbol of Soviet oppression. In 2007, when it was announced that the statue would be moved to the outskirts of the city, Russian speakers in the city rioted, inflamed by the Russian-speaking media outlets who reported falsely that the statue was due to be destroyed. Over 26 and 27 April there were riots, looting and cyber attacks. Further fanning the flames of violence, Russian-language media outlets did not report the violent riots, but instead reported that peaceful Russian protesters were being targeted by the Estonian police.

The situation escalated when banks, the media and government services were the target of widescale DDoS attacks: research from NATO suggests that one to two million infected bots were used in the attack, running through 175 jurisdictions, to flood Estonian websites and online services with traffic that would make the services go offline (DDoS attacks and bots are covered in Chapter 4). NATO note that 174 jurisdictions supported Estonia in resolving the attacks and the Russian Federation alone did not.[5]

This activity disrupted cash machines and online banking, took government email out of action and prevented Estonian news outlets from operating. The campaign lasted for three weeks and had a profound impact on Estonia, partly because the activity was unprecedented (there had never been such a coordinated cyber attack on a country before) with, at one point, 58 separate botnet attacks hitting Estonia in one day.[6] In a statement made at the time, the Estonian Foreign Minister Urmas Paet said that the 'virtual, psychological and real attacks' were coordinated actions from Russia against Estonia and, by extension, the European Union.[7] Russia denies any role in the cyber attack and attribution of the attacks proved difficult, because they were seemingly carried out by individuals under their own steam and using their own personal resources.

The activity was also unprecedented because of the impact it had. Estonia had become one of the most digitized countries in the world, with public services delivered through the internet, including election voting (Estonia was the first country in the world to offer internet voting).

Estonia's response to the attack is to be commended. The country drew on its information security community to respond to the attack and to build resilience into its future approach. The incident galvanized policymakers, and so in May 2008, the Estonian Ministry of Defence implemented a cyber security strategy and the NATO Cooperative Cyber Defence Centre of Excellence was established in Tallinn. In the decade and more that has passed since the attack, Estonia has become recognized as one of the leading countries in cyber security, advising other states on the subject. Rather than moving away from its digital infrastructure, Estonia has strengthened its e-government systems and sought to make its population more aware of cyber security: the Organisation for Economic Co-operation and Development (OECD) describes Estonia as the most technically advanced government in the world.[8] One progression that Estonia has developed as part of its e-Estonia initiative is that of data embassies, in which digital copies of key national data are held under Estonian jurisdiction in Luxembourg.

A year after the attack in Estonia, the country of Georgia was targeted with the first-ever combined cyber and kinetic attacks, as part of a war between Georgia and Russia over South Ossetia. For the digital element, many of the same techniques and computers that were used in the Estonia attack were seen again in the activities targeting Georgia. The website of the Georgian President was hacked, along with websites of news outlets. Georgian websites were subject to DDoS attacks and deface-ment, and internet traffic was re-routed through servers in Russia and Turkey and subsequently blocked. In terms of the kinetic warfare, it has been estimated by the European Union that 800 people lost their lives, across both sides, over the five days of physical warfare.[9]

Stuxnet

The blurring of lines between cyber and physical attacks is seen more at the nation-state level than any other dimension of cyber security. One such case is Stuxnet, understood to be the first malware that caused physical destruction. This made Stuxnet unprecedented; a game-changer not just in how it crossed the kinetic boundary, but also in terms of its sophistication, with Kaspersky Lab estimating that it would have taken a team of ten coders two to three years to create it. It targeted 'airgapped' systems (systems not connected to the internet) and was transmitted mainly via USB sticks. In fact, Stuxnet had a very specific target: the centrifuges that spin nuclear material at Natanz, Iran's main nuclear enrichment facility. It was identified in 2010, hiding in the systems of the power plants and signalling to the operating system that everything was normal. Stuxnet set the country's nuclear production programme back by at least 18 months when it destroyed 1,000 of the 5,000 centrifuges at Natanz.[10] Attribution of Stuxnet was challenging, but in 2012, the *New York Times* published an in-depth report claiming what many suspected, that it was the work of the United States, under President Obama's orders, in collaboration with Israel.[11]

What the creators of Stuxnet apparently did not intend or expect was that the worm would escape from Natanz. Stuxnet spread to an engineer's computer when it was connected to the centrifuges due to an error in the code; when that computer was then connected to the internet, the worm began self-replicating around the world.[12] Stuxnet was the first cyber weapon and illustrated that cyber weapons are not (yet) like kinetic weapons. With traditional, kinetic warfare, weaponry has become more precise and targeted, resulting in less collateral damage. In cyber

THE PHYSICAL SIDE OF CYBER SECURITY

warfare, it is much more difficult to make weaponry that is precise, targeted and contained, with no risk of collateral damage.

WannaCry

We have been reminded of this reality many times since Stuxnet, not least with WannaCry. In Chapter 3, we covered what happened when WannaCry hit and how the attack was thwarted; now we will explore the nation-state dimensions. WannaCry propagated through EternalBlue, an exploit that takes advantage of a vulnerability in Microsoft's Server Message Block (SMB; a method that allows for shared access to files, printers and ports on a network). The exploit was discovered, or perhaps even created, by the US National Security Agency (NSA) and kept secret by the Agency, not informing Microsoft of it for five years until a hacking group named the Shadow Brokers revealed they had possession of it. If an intelligence agency creates or discovers an exploit, they may be motivated to keep it secret so they can use it in operations against other nation states. Many people criticize this practice, especially in the wake of WannaCry and other attacks that utilize EternalBlue, but it seems a fact of life that intelligence agencies will conduct themselves this way. Spies are going to spy!

From 2016 to 2017, the Shadow Brokers released highly classified NSA data that dated no later than 2013. The data included the EternalBlue exploit, along with details of major vulnerabilities in Cisco routers, Linux mail servers and more, and came from the NSA's hacking group, Tailored Access Operations (TAO, also known as the Equation Group).

The timeline of events was as follows:

August 2016: The Shadow Brokers announce possession of TAO/NSA classified data and attempt to auction it.

January 2017: The Shadow Brokers publish screenshots that show a list of exploit tools, including EternalBlue.

March 2017: Microsoft patch the vulnerability that can be exploited by EternalBlue.

April 2017: The Shadow Brokers release all of the tools shown in the screenshot they shared in January, including EternalBlue.

May 2017: WannaCry hits.

It is largely a matter of speculation as to who the Shadow Brokers are, but many agree that the group operate at the nation-state level and that the most likely state is Russia.

The NSA faced criticism for withholding information regarding the vulnerability that was leveraged by the EternalBlue exploit. Since then, the NSA has – for the first time – been attributed with publicly disclosing a vulnerability that they discovered: on 14 January 2020, Microsoft released a patch for vulnerability CVE-2020-0601, which they attributed to the NSA.[13]

The Russian invasion of Ukraine

Cyber war, but perhaps not as we expected it. With the brutal land invasion of Ukraine, Russia also continued a campaign of cyberwar against the country. In fact, as cybersecurity expert Kenneth Geers highlighted, Russia launched cyber attacks on Ukraine 10 days ahead of the physical invasion.[14]

Ukraine suffered a threefold growth in cyber attacks over 2022, with Russian hacking at times deployed in combination with missile strikes.[15] There have been numerous attempts by Russia to bring down elements of Ukraine's critical national infrastructure. However, having long been the target of Russian cyber attacks – and with support from the West – Ukraine has been more prepared and more resilient than many feared.

There are differences of opinion in the analysis of the cyber element of the Russian invasion of Ukraine. Some argue that there is a full-on cyber war occurring, while others conclude that the offensive cyber capabilities of Russia are clearly not as powerful as perhaps they once were.

According to Geers, Ukraine's ability to maintain online connectivity has been a crucial element of its success:

> In this cyber war, information operations have turned out to be much more important than computer hacking. And Zelensky's ability to stay online and in touch with the world is impressive. He is the voice of the country, and that could be decisive in this war.[16]

Lindy Cameron, CEO of the UK NCSC, described the Russian attacks on Ukraine as the 'most sustained and intensive cyber campaign on record', concluding that this shows 'a strong and effective cyber defense can be mounted, even against an adversary as well prepared and resourced as the Russian Federation'.[17]

The threat to critical national infrastructure in Ukraine remains present, and allies continue to brace themselves.

Companies and nation-state-level attacks

It is not simply governments who are targeted at the nation-state level. In an effort to cause destabilization, state-owned and private companies that are linked to nation states can become the target of nation-state-level activity.

Saudi Aramco

On 15 August 2012, one of the most destructive computer viruses ever seen sabotaged Saudi Aramco, the state-owned oil company of Saudi Arabia. The data on three-quarters of Saudi Aramco's computers (35,000 in total) was completely destroyed, and replaced with an image of a burning American flag. Aramco shut down the internal corporate network, disabling email and internet access, in an attempt to contain the virus, called Shamoon. Oil production was segregated on the network, and so unaffected, but the business side of Aramco was completely disconnected, with a return to pen and paper, typewriters and fax machines. Recovery took months.

The attack was claimed by a hacking group calling themselves 'Cutting Sword of Justice', who said they were motivated by Saudi policies in the Middle East, although many believe this is a ruse and the true culprits are Iran, potentially in retaliation for Stuxnet, using lessons learned from the attack. Much like Stuxnet, it is suspected that an insider was fundamental to the Shamoon infection of Aramco, initiating it by plugging in a USB stick containing the virus.

As the state-owned national oil company of Saudi Arabia, it is not surprising that Saudi Aramco would be targeted by nation-state actors. However, we also see private companies that are not state-owned being caught up in nation-state-level activity.

Notpetya

The shipping giant Maersk is responsible for approximately one-fifth of the world's shipping capacity, carrying tens of millions of tons of cargo around the world. On 27 June 2017, computers across Maersk were infected by NotPetya. Computers shut down, phones stopped working, access gates locked and the vast majority of employees were told to go home until further notice.

Maersk was caught up in a huge attack using the malware NotPetya, which has been identified as a tool in the Russian war with Ukraine. NotPetya is linked to, but not the same as, the ransomware Petya, which spread via email attachments; NotPetya masqueraded as ransomware but was irreversible, intended to destroy not extort. It was built on EternalBlue and Mimikatz (a penetration testing tool that can pull passwords out of computer memory and use them to hack into other machines using the same username and passwords). The combination of these two tools was powerful, meaning that computers that were not patched against ExternalBlue could be hacked and then, via use of Mimikatz, those that were patched could be accessed and infected.[18]

Ukraine was the first to be hit with NotPetya, and was hit with the majority of infections, with victims including banks, energy firms and Borispol airport in Kiev. This is not the first time Ukraine has been subject to cyber attacks at the nation-state level: it has been a target of cyber attacks in parallel to Russian military intervention in the country since 2014. During this time, companies running Ukraine's power grid have been targeted, resulting in blackouts that affected hundreds of thousands of citizens for up to six hours.

Although the NotPetya malware is understood to have been specifically targeting Ukraine, the malware did not stop at the country's borders, but soon spread around the world. NotPetya indiscriminately and permanently encrypted the hard drives of tens of thousands of computers – not only in Maersk, but also the pharmaceutical company Merck and the courier delivery service FedEx – costing each company hundreds of millions of dollars. The United States White House has identified the Russian military as the source of NotPetya, whilst describing it as the most destructive and costly cyber attack so far experienced.[19]

Misinformation and disinformation

It is common for nation-state cyber activity to be covert and challenging to attribute. However, when that activity is not only about code, but also about misinformation and influencing hearts and minds, it becomes an even greater challenge to identify and confront.

In October 2016, the United States formally accused Russia of interfering in the elections earlier that year, in which Donald Trump was voted in as president. A joint statement from the Department of Homeland Security and the Director of National Intelligence claimed that the Russian administration, at its most senior level, was responsible for hacking Democratic party officials and stealing 19,000 emails, which were then leaked to the press via Wikileaks (linking back to the chapter on social engineering, the emails were reportedly compromised via a spear-phishing email attack in which the credentials of officials were compromised). At the time of the hack, it was claimed by Guccifer 2.0, who maintained they were an independent hacker but who many security experts and US officials believe is the public persona of a group within Russia's Main Intelligence Directorate (known by its Russian acronym, GRU). This hacking group is known by many names, including Advanced Persistent Threat 28 (APT28), Fancy Bear and Sofacy Group.

In 2017, the US Office of the Director of National Intelligence released a report which claimed that Vladimir Putin, the Russian President, ordered a campaign to influence the 2016 US election, which included discrediting Trump's political rival, Hillary Clinton. This alleged interference included not only the hacking of Democrat emails, but also a misinformation campaign conducted online through social media, intended to influence how people voted in the election.

In 2019, the long-awaited conclusion to a US independent inquiry, the *Report on the Investigation into Russian Interference in the 2016 Presidential Election* (known as the Mueller report), was published. The 448-page report detailed occasions when the US President had attempted to obstruct the investigation and welcomed the potential for the hacked, leaked emails to damage Clinton, but the report did not establish whether the Trump campaign criminally conspired with Russia to influence the 2016 election. In 2018, thirteen Russians were indicted by the US for attempting to manipulate US voters using social media in the run-up to the 2016 election. The Russian Internet Research Agency (IRA) allegedly conducted extensive research into tactics that would influence the election, stole identities of real Americans on social media, created fake accounts and paid for political adverts on platforms such as Facebook, using virtual private networks to route their traffic through the US so they could go undetected.

In July 2020, the UK Parliament's Intelligence and Security Committee released its report on Russia's influence in UK politics. The report concluded that the UK government had failed to assess whether Russia had interfered in the Brexit referendum and described Russian interference in the UK as the 'new normal'. According to the report, the UK had time to develop more robust defences against Russian hacking and misinformation: the committee concluded that Russia's efforts to sway voters in Scotland ahead of the 2014 independence referendum marked the first known attempt to interfere in the democratic processes of a Western country. However, the report concludes that it was only after Russia's 'hack and leak' operation against the US Democrats (with the emails made public one month after the Brexit referendum) that the UK government realized the threat that Russia could pose in this area.[20]

State-on-state activity, including kinetic warfare and attempts to influence elections, is nothing new. However, the internet has opened up potential for more covert, more scalable and more deniable activity and has complicated issues of sovereignty, jurisdiction and attribution. Cyber activities at the nation-state level are complex, with attacks that are not simply intended to directly impact governments but include insidious activity that is intended to destabilize and disrupt. Over the last decade, we have seen more nation-state cyber activity and we can be sure that cyberspace will increasingly be used by nation states as part of geopolitical conflict.

Notes

1 Schmitt, M N (ed) (2017) *Tallinn Manual 2.0 on International Law Applicable to Cyber Operations*, Cambridge University Press, Cambridge
2 Moussouris, K (2017) Serious progress made on the Wassenaar Arrangement for global cybersecurity, The Hill, 17 December, https://thehill.com/opinion/cybersecurity/365352-serious-progress-made-on-the-wassenaar-arrangement-for-global (archived at https://perma.cc/Z77F-BBVY)

3 United States Department of State Bureau of Diplomatic Security (2011) *History of the Bureau of Diplomatic Security of the United States Department of State*, https://2009-2017.state.gov/documents/organization/176589.pdf (archived at https://perma.cc/HS4J-HD6V)

4 Hills, M (2019) *Hybrid Threats: A strategic communications perspective: 2007 cyber attacks on Estonia*, NATO Strategic Communications, www.stratcomcoe.org/publications (archived at https://perma.cc/9P4T-63VB)

5 Hills, M (2019) *Hybrid Threats: A Strategic Communications Perspective: 2007 Cyber Attacks on Estonia*, NATO Strategic Communications, www.stratcomcoe.org/publications (archived at https://perma.cc/9P4T-63VB)

6 Davis, J (2007) Hackers take down the most wired country in Europe, Wired, 21 August, www.wired.com/2007/08/ff-estonia (archived at https://perma.cc/DEJ7-HS4E)

7 Pau, A (2007) Statement by the Foreign Minister Urmas Paet, Eesti Päevaleht, 1 May, https://epl.delfi.ee/eesti/statement-by-the-foreign-minister-urmas-paet?id=51085399 (archived at https://perma.cc/UM5L-WSZG)

8 OECD Observatory of Public Sector Innovation and Mohammed Bin Rashid Centre for Government Innovation (2018) Embracing innovation in government: Global trends 2018, www.oecd.org/innovation/innovative-government/innovation2018.htm (archived at https://perma.cc/VR4X-GEGW)

9 European Convention on Human Rights (2009) *Independent International Fact-Finding Mission on the Conflict in Georgia*, www.echr.coe.int/Documents/HUDOC_38263_08_Annexes_ENG.pdf (archived at https://perma.cc/F28V-UEPE)

10 Albright, D, Brannan, P and Walrond, C (2011) Stuxnet malware and Natanz: Update of ISIS December 22, 2010 report, Institute for Science and International Security, https://isis-online.org/uploads/isis-reports/documents/stuxnet_FEP_22Dec2010.pdf (archived at https://perma.cc/NN7G-V9UH)

11 Sanger, D (2012) Obama order sped up wave of cyberattacks against Iran, *New York Times*, 1 June, www.nytimes.com/2012/06/01/world/middleeast/obama-ordered-wave-of-cyberattacks-against-iran.html (archived at https://perma.cc/LG72-29MS)

12 Sanger, D (2012) Obama order sped up wave of cyberattacks against Iran, *New York Times*, 1 June, www.nytimes.com/2012/06/01/world/middleeast/obama-ordered-wave-of-cyberattacks-against-iran.html (archived at https://perma.cc/LG72-29MS)

13 FC (2020) The first official NSA exploit (CVE-2020-0601) (blog), Cygenta, 15 January, https://blog.cygenta.co.uk/first-nsa-exploit/ (archived at https://perma.cc/2LRK-8BZY)

14   https://www.theregister.com/2022/05/13/cyberspace_is_first_theatre_of_war/
      (archived at https://perma.cc/M2D7-PLZC)
15   https://www.theguardian.com/world/2023/jan/19/cyber-attacks-have-tripled-
      in-past-year-says-ukraine-cybersecurity-agency (archived at https://perma.cc/
      EG5N-GC6G)
16   https://therecord.media/qa-kenneth-geers-on-the-cyber-war-between-ukraine-
      and-russia/ (archived at https://perma.cc/UMV9-FPP7)
17   https://www.infosecurity-magazine.com/news/ncsc-learn-ukraine-cyber-
      defenses/ (archived at https://perma.cc/U6TM-ZB4E)
18   Greenberg, A (2019) *Sandworm: A new era of cyberwar and the hunt for the
      Kremlin's most dangerous hackers*, Doubleday, New York
19   Greenberg, A (2018) The White House blames Russia for NotPetya, the 'most
      costly cyberattack in history', Wired, 15 February, www.wired.com/story/
      white-house-russia-notpetya-attribution (archived at https://perma.cc/7276-
      WX5M)
20   https://isc.independent.gov.uk/wp-content/uploads/2021/03/CCS207_
      CCS0221966010-001_Russia-Report-v02-Web_Accessible.pdf (archived at
      https://perma.cc/59GL-8VL6)

PART FIVE

The future of cyber security and what it means for your career

CHAPTER ELEVEN

Cyber security in different industries

When you first hear the term 'cyber security' you would be forgiven for thinking that it's only something that governments, banks and big corporations need to consider. And, of course, those industries absolutely do need to embrace cyber security – but they're not the only ones. Cyber security considerations apply to all sorts of different organizations and industries, including ones that you might not expect.

Celebrity, entertainment and pop culture

Taylor Swift

Have you ever wondered how someone like Taylor Swift manages cyber security? Success in the music industry relies on many things, and one of those is music being released at the time and in the way intended. If songs or albums are leaked before their release date, it could cost the artist and their record label a good deal of money and, potentially, damage the career of the artist. According to news reports, Taylor Swift (or, certainly, her team) is very aware of this and takes a number of steps to manage her most valuable data: her upcoming music.

It is reported that when backing dancers are performing in the filming of Taylor Swift's music videos, they are not performing to the actual track that will be the subject of the video. To ensure that her music is only heard by those who absolutely need to hear it, and apparently limit the possibility of someone secretly recording and releasing the music before the official release date, Swift's backing dancers perform to 'click tracks' which play the correct beat of the relevant track rather than the track itself.[1] That way, the dancers are performing to the correct rhythm but without being exposed to the music.

Reports suggest that it this is not an isolated example with regards to keeping Swift's music secure, but rather part of an overall approach. Ed Sheeran has commented on the measures that Swift's team took to protect her music, when they collaborated on the song *Everything Has Changed* on her album *Red*. According to Sheeran, he listened to the song once, when a member of Swift's team met him. The track was apparently the only song on an iPad, which was stored in a locked briefcase; Sheeran listened to it once before acknowledging that he was happy with it, and the iPad was then locked up and taken back.[2] This shows a considered approach to the cyber security of Swift's intellectual property. Swift's team are keeping a careful chain of custody of the music, not sending it via email, which can be vulnerable to hacking, and from what Sheeran has said, possibly even keeping the song on a so-called 'clean' device, one that has not been used to access the internet or store other data.

It is not just Swift's digital security that her team take so seriously, but also her physical security as well. In 2018, it was reported that kiosks showing rehearsal clips of Taylor Swift, set up outside her concert venue, were more than they first appeared. When concertgoers watched the clips of Swift being played at the kiosks, their images were taken, and facial recognition scans were performed to determine if any of the attendees were known stalkers of Swift.[3] This may seem extreme, and it certainly raises questions regarding the balance of personal security for one individual compared to the personal privacy of others, but it represents how celebrities can (and do) embrace the latest digital technologies as part of their approach to security.

Kim Kardashian

Physical security is, of course, an issue that people in the public eye have long been aware of. However, these issues have been brought more to the fore with the advent of greater connectivity over the internet and social media technology, meaning people with a high profile are more accessible to the rest of us compared to even a few decades ago. In 2016, the Kardashians re-evaluated their use of social media after Kim Kardashian was attacked while staying in Paris. Kardashian was robbed at gunpoint, with the criminals stealing $10 million worth of jewellery. The alleged leader of the criminal group told French police that he and his team were able to pull off the attack by using information she had shared on social media.[4] Kardashian had shown pictures of expensive jewels on social media, commenting that they were not fake, and her posts also revealed information about her whereabouts and movements whilst in Paris. This is, of course, not to blame Kardashian for the attack: she was a victim of criminal action and suffered what, by all accounts, must have been a very traumatizing experience. The case does highlight, however, the fact that criminals use social media as a tool in their activities. This is something for us all to be aware of, but particularly people with a high profile. It means that cyber security is of central importance to celebrities, to protect not just their data security and finances, but also their physical security.

Caitlyn Jenner

And there are plenty of examples from the Kardashian empire. When Caitlyn Jenner transitioned gender this was of course a huge news story – which means cyber security was central to it (as we first covered in Chapter 8). *Vanity Fair* had the very exclusive first public interview and photoshoot with Jenner after her transition, which involved a great deal of security to maintain the exclusivity and prevent details, such as photographs, from leaking. Extra security was reportedly hired for the photoshoot, with everyone on site forced to be without mobile phones to prevent them from taking photographs. The article and the photographs were contained on only one computer, which was never connected to the internet, with all of the data put on a flash drive every night and deleted from the machine itself. The story was hand-delivered to the printers, rather than risked over the internet.[5]

Although such security measures may seem extreme, they actually make perfect sense. For journalists and the media, maintaining all aspects of cyber security is important: confidentiality, integrity and (discussed in the next section) availability. Confidentiality of information is obviously important, to ensure that any scoops are maintained; loss of confidentiality could affect the journalist or media outlet in financial terms but also damage their reputation. Integrity of information is crucial, to prevent information being altered: imagine the damage that could be done if information for news stories was changed without the media outlet being aware, with malicious intent. This would give a whole new meaning to 'fake news', with potential far-reaching social, political and economic consequences if a reputable news source was manipulated into publishing misinformation.

Journalism and the media

We saw an example of the impact that misinformation, spread by a cyber security incident, can have in 2013 when the Associated Press (AP) Twitter account was hacked. A tweet was sent from the hacked account saying that two explosions had occurred at the White House, and Barack Obama, who was President of the United States at the time, was injured. Although the information was immediately corrected by AP employees on Twitter and the tweet was deleted as soon as it was discovered, the spreading of misinformation from a reputable source led to a large, albeit brief, drop in the US stock market (a 143-point fall in the Dow Jones industrial average).[6] Although the market recovered within a few minutes, it highlights the interdependencies between social media, news outlets and economic and social structures of society; and, crucially, the importance of security within all of this.

The third strand of the cyber security triad is availability. There can be a notion that cyber security is all about locking information down, but in fact making sure that information which *should* be available, *is* available when it is needed is fundamental to cyber security. In October 2019, many websites and organizations in the country of Georgia were targeted in a cyber attack, including two TV broadcasters, Imedi TV and Maestro, and the websites for local newspapers. Over 15,000 websites were defaced, made possible by the attackers compromising a web hosting provider. Many concluded that the attack was the work of nation-state-sponsored hackers, with speculation that it was a repeat of the 2008 cyber attack on Georgia, at a time when conflict between Russia and Georgia was escalating (see page 166 for more information). In attacking media outlets, this cyber attack was targeting the availability of information, cutting people off from sources that would update them on the news, including news on the attacks themselves.

Sport

In 2019, Deloitte estimated that the European football market was worth £25.1 billion.[7] In 2020, the UK National Cyber Security Centre reported that at least 70 per cent of sports organizations have experienced a cyber incident or breach; 30 per cent of those incidents caused direct financial damage, with the biggest single loss over £4 million.[8] The NCSC highlight that most attacks on sports organizations will be carried out by financially motivated cyber criminals, with a few targeted attacks at the state level. In 2017, the BBC reported on the UK Football Association's concern that sensitive information could be exposed during the 2018 World Cup in Russia.[9] This concern was in light of a hack by the Russian group commonly known as Fancy Bear, in which documents were leaked that indicated 160 football players had used banned medicines at the 2010 World Cup.[10] When sport means so much to national identity and national economies, of course it has the potential to be caught in the crossfire of nation-state hacking.

There is a lot of money at stake at the national level of sport, and of course a great deal of money at stake for individual clubs. In 2019, news emerged that Liverpool Football Club had paid Manchester City a £1 million settlement in response to a complaint from Manchester City that their scouting system had been hacked. The settlement was paid confidentially, in 2013, a year after three former Manchester City scouts joined Liverpool Football Club. Manchester City reportedly used the services of digital forensics experts to identify whether their system had been accessed in a way that was not approved; the allegations were not taken to court and the settlement was made without the Premier League being informed or Liverpool Football Club accepting any liability for wrongdoing.[11] Details on upcoming talented players, players' injuries, team tactics, planned negotiations and more must be confidential – just like other industries, information is hugely valuable for football.

Social media and influencers

The internet and online systems have become central to many businesses, and indeed to society as a whole, which is why cyber security is, in turn, so fundamental to organizations and individuals. The influencer marketing industry is worth billions of pounds and so, combined with its reliance on connected technology, it is inevitably a target of cybercrime. In November 2019, UK fashion designer Bree Kotomah's Instagram account was compromised, which led to the account being shut down and, as her Instagram account was essentially her shop, the business ceased to function for months until Kotomah restructured how she ran her company.[12]

Fake Elon Musk YouTube Scams

In just over one week in 2022, cyber criminals scammed YouTube viewers out of $243,000 worth of bitcoin and $9,000 worth of Ethereum.[13] And, this was just one week among many in which scammers compromised YouTube accounts with large numbers of subscribers and made the hijacked accounts look like official Tesla channels. The accounts then shared deepfake videos of Elon Musk, making it appear as if Musk was promoting cryptocurrency investment schemes. At the same time, official adverts were broadcast also showing similar deepfake videos. Viewers are encouraged to 'invest', but it's all a scam and any cryptocurrency which is sent is lost to the criminals. Musk himself criticized YouTube for seeming to be 'nonstop scam ads'.[14]

This was not the first time that Elon Musk's image and status had been hijacked by cyber criminals to launch cryptocurrency scams. In 2021, analysts at Whale Alert reported that these 'giveaway scammers' made a profit of $98 million.[15] This included one victim who was convinced to part with £400,000 worth of bitcoin under the promise that his return would double. This individual described the loss as having 'thrown away the gamechanger for my family, my early retirement fund and all the upcoming holidays with my kids'.[16]

WHAT ARE DEEPFAKES?

Deepfakes first emerged in 2017 and, in the last few years, have become very advanced – and much more widespread – very quickly. Deepfakes are video, images or audio that have been manipulated to replace the original person with someone else's likeness. They use artificial intelligence to generate fake images, video or audio combined with deep neural networks, which are a type of AI algorithm that finds patterns in large sets of data. Hence the name 'deepfakes'.

Creating a convincing deepfake video requires a lot of data, as the image of the 'target' must be swapped in every frame of the video. Creating this involves running thousands of images through an AI algorithm called an encoder. The encoder can map the two faces and learn their similarities using lots of images of the two people who are being swapped. A decoder, which is a second AI algorithm, is then used to recover the two faces and swap them.

Academic experts at University College London have rated deepfakes as the most serious crime threat posed by artificial intelligence.[17] Let's take a deeper look at the threat posed by these fakes.

There are different levels to the threat posed. At the individual level, there is of course the potential for deepfakes to be used in false allegations, leading to reputational damage and more. At the organizational level, there is reputational damage to consider as well as the social engineering potential, for example with deepfakes used to impersonate the target's boss, asking the target to transfer a sum of money due to an emergency. Our increasing use of video communications and voice messaging in recent years brings with it many benefits, but also widens the scope for criminals to hijack these channels with deepfakes.

Deepfakes also pose a challenge at the social level and political level. Public figures such as politicians, celebrities, influencers and high-profile business leaders are an obvious target for the use of deepfakes. Their high profile and sphere of influence already makes public figures a target and, of course, there is generally a lot of images and audio recordings available for high-profile individuals, making deepfakes easier to generate.

In March 2022, we had a warning of what may be to come. A video, apparently of Ukrainian president Volodymyr Zelensky, appeared online. It was a rather unconvincing deepfake in which the image of Zelensky was presented as announcing a surrender to Russia's invasion. The video was not as technically convincing as many deepfakes and was quickly rebutted by a real video by Zelensky and swift social media response, but it appears to be the first weaponization of deepfake technology in a war. Ukraine was prepared for the use of deepfake technology against them; we must all be aware of how such technology could be used to manipulate us – at the personal, organizational or social and political level.

When it comes to deepfakes, just like other social engineering scams, we can't necessarily believe our eyes and ears, so we must verify before we trust.

Small and medium enterprises

The targeting of social media influencers shows that it is not just large organizations that find themselves harmed by cyber insecurity and the activities of cyber criminals. The Federation of Small Businesses has found that cybercrime is costing the small business community in the UK billions of pounds a year, with 20 per cent of small UK businesses reporting suffering a cyber attack in the years 2017–19 and the average direct cost of an individual attack for each business being £1,300.[18] Small businesses are most commonly caught up in phishing email scams, infections of malware and ransomware. Small businesses are often surprised when they are the victim of a cyber attack, often because there is an assumption that cybercrime is targeted and, alongside this, that only large businesses would be targeted. In reality, cyber criminals often cast a wide net; this is easy with attacks such as phishing scams and credential stuffing (described in Chapter 4).

Cyber criminals are able to send a large number of phishing emails at a time or harvest a great deal of passwords in one go, using computer programs, and as small businesses often do not have the same cyber security defences as larger businesses, they are an attractive target. Small and large organizations alike can find that they are caught up in a cyber attack not because they are the direct target, but because they are the *supplier* of the true target. This was the case with the US retailer Target, who were breached via their refrigeration, heating and air conditioning company; the breach allegedly led to the Chief Information Officer and Chief Executive Officer of Target resigning after costs reached $162 million.

Education

Education is another sector that has found itself, perhaps unexpectedly, the target of cybercrime. Universities are often home to a great deal of intellectual property, and research and development data, as well as large amounts of funds and personal data. With a decentralized structure and many different stakeholders (academics, professional staff, researchers and students), universities can be challenging organizations to secure. Traditionally in many businesses, there is a culture of 'top down', centralized authority, with an acceptance that leadership set the rules and everyone else falls in line, to greater and lesser extents. In universities, there are often distinct schools and departments that operate fairly independently of the central university function. Academics and researchers have an authority that can be challenging to 'rule over' in the traditional sense: it may be hard for a chief information security officer in a university to tell a leading academic that they should not store sensitive research data on a USB stick or email it to their personal email address because of the cyber security risks, as the culture of academia is not structured in the top-down way of many other organizations.

Whilst it is in the best interest of the academic, as well as the university as whole, to protect the data, the CISO needs to persuade the academic rather than rely on institutional authority.

In July 2019, Lancaster University reported that it had been the victim of a cyber attack, which involved phishing emails.[19] The students' record system was accessed and some students had their student record and identification documents breached. At the same time, the names, addresses, telephone numbers and email addresses of undergraduate applicants were stolen, enabling the cyber criminals to send phishing emails, with fake university invoices, to some of the applicants.

This example highlights an important issue: we can sometimes underestimate the value of our email addresses, with a tendency for many of us to share them widely. Email addresses represent value to cyber criminals and fraudsters because they can use these to contact us with phishing emails. If a cyber criminal is able to access a list of email addresses, especially combined with information such as the university that they have applied to, they can use this information to quickly send a convincing phishing email that will be profitable for them if only one person takes the bait. If you have applied for a university, are expecting to make a payment to them and receive an email which comes from a university account (or looks very convincingly as if it comes from a legitimate account), wouldn't you pay the invoice?

Personal data, the need to keep operating and low IT budgets are factors that also make the education sector vulnerable to cyber attacks. A group going by the name Vice Society have reportedly been behind the compromise of numerous schools in the UK and US, for example leaking confidential information from 14 UK schools in January 2023. This information included child passport scans, special needs information and staff contract details.[20] In an alert published in September 2022, the FBI referred to Vice Society as 'disproportionately targeting the education sector with ransomware attacks', suggesting that they generally gain access to the networks via compromised credentials before they exfiltrate data and then deploy ransomware.[21]

CONVEYANCING FRAUD

In 2017, the Solicitors Regulation Authority (SRA) reported client losses of £10 million in relation to conveyancing fraud, which they also refer to as Friday afternoon fraud.[22] In this attack, cyber criminals insert themselves in the middle of communications between a solicitor and a house buyer while a purchase of a house is taking place. By compromising the account of the solicitor or using an email address that appears very similar to the solicitor's legitimate one, the criminals pose as the solicitor and provide the house buyer with bank details that the house deposit should be paid to. The house buyer transfers the deposit, believing that they are transferring the money for the purchase of the house to the legitimate solicitor, the money goes to the criminal's bank account details and the solicitor is unaware that any of this is taking place. As is the case with many social engineering attacks, there is a trend for them to be carried out on a Friday afternoon, when people are in a rush to complete transactions and when the criminal has a weekend to evade detection and hide the money via proxy accounts and money mules.

In January 2023, *Which* helped a couple who had lost £80,500 in a case of conveyancing fraud. While in the process of buying a house, the couple received a phone call from criminals posing as their solicitors to arrange the transfer of funds. They transferred £80,500 through the Halifax banking app only to discover, days later, that they had been scammed. Halifax originally only agreed to return half of the money, until *Which* contacted them and requested a review on behalf of the couple. Halifax then returned the full amount, concluding that the scam had been hard to identify.

Such reimbursements are not the only good news when it comes to conveyancing fraud. It seems that greater awareness of the scams has led to a reduction in the amount of successful attacks. The SRA has reported a reduction in losses every year since a peak of £10 million in 2017. This is apart from an increase to £2.3 million in 2021, around half of which was unfortunately due to a single fraudulent transaction. In the first 10 months of 2022, losses fell to £700,000.[23] Each case is more than we would like, and can be financially and emotionally devastating for victims, but seeing the losses reduce is progress: a sign that raising awareness and encouraging vigilance can make a large impact.

These are just a few examples of the careers, industries and areas where cyber security is a highly relevant concern – there are many more. Arguably, it is any industry that needs these skills – not just big business. Wherever money or information is at stake, we need to guard against the activities of cyber criminals.

Notes

1 Taylor Swift (2018) End Game – behind the scenes (online video), https://youtu.be/VA7Y_Psp5l4 (archived at https://perma.cc/A558-BJ9N)

2 Prakash, N (2017) Ed Sheeran explains how Taylor Swift keeps her music from leaking, *TeenVogue*, 10 February, www.teenvogue.com/story/ed-sheeran-reveals-how-taylor-swift-keeps-music-from-leaking (archived at https://perma.cc/E62P-SZUB)

3 Knopper, S (2018) Why Taylor Swift is using facial recognition at concerts, *Rolling Stone*, 13 December, www.rollingstone.com/music/music-news/taylor-swift-facial-recognition-concerts-768741 (archived at https://perma.cc/PR5E-X5NN)

4 Bryant, K (2017) Kim Kardashian's alleged robber confirms social media helped him plan heist, *Vanity Fair*, 30 January, www.vanityfair.com/style/2017/01/kim-kardashian-paris-robbery-social-media-heist (archived at https://perma.cc/T9LC-5UGA)

5   Miller, J (2015) The inside story of Caitlyn Jenner's historic Vanity Fair cover, *Vanity Fair*, 27 July, www.vanityfair.com/hollywood/2015/07/caitlyn-jenner-documentary (archived at https://perma.cc/LFX8-B4AZ)

6   Moore, H and Roberts, D (2013) AP Twitter hack causes panic on Wall Street and sends Dow plunging, *Guardian*, 23 April, www.theguardian.com/business/2013/apr/23/ap-tweet-hack-wall-street-freefall (archived at https://perma.cc/F6B3-ZDND)

7   Deloitte (2019) Annual review of football finance 2019, www2.deloitte.com/uk/en/pages/sports-business-group/articles/annual-review-of-football-finance.html (archived at https://perma.cc/SUS3-7X4H)

8   https://www.ncsc.gov.uk/files/Cyber-threat-to-sports-organisations.pdf (archived at https://perma.cc/55SW-TBQZ)

9   Conway, R (2017) World Cup 2018: FA increases cyber security over hacking concerns, BBC Sport, 11 September, www.bbc.co.uk/sport/football/41230542 (archived at https://perma.cc/X6KH-EF55)

10 BBC (2017) Fancy Bears: Hackers name footballers given 2010 World Cup TUEs, BBC Sport, 22 August, www.bbc.co.uk/sport/football/41011854 (archived at https://perma.cc/MHR9-X8A6)

11 Ziegler, M and Dickinson, M (2019) Liverpool paid Manchester City £1m 'spy' settlement, *The Times*, 21 September, www.thetimes.co.uk/edition/sport/liverpool-paid-manchester-city-1m-spy-settlement-mxkns7mb6 (archived at https://perma.cc/4GHN-PX7G)

12 Russon, M-A (2019) My Instagram got hacked and I lost my business, BBC Business, 19 August, www.bbc.co.uk/news/business-49397038 (archived at https://perma.cc/K66Y-BNFH)

13 https://www.bbc.co.uk/news/technology-61749120 (archived at https://perma.cc/EFH9-8FTW)

14 https://twitter.com/elonmusk/status/1534196611978383361 (archived at https://perma.cc/PWP2-AP56)

15 ibid

16 https://www.bbc.co.uk/news/technology-56402378 (archived at https://perma.cc/DJ5M-7Z3W)

17 https://www.ucl.ac.uk/news/2020/aug/deepfakes-ranked-most-serious-ai-crime-threat (archived at https://perma.cc/QC37-APLY)

18 Federation of Small Businesses (2019) Small firms suffer close to 10,000 cyber-attacks daily, FSB Press Release, 5 August, www.fsb.org.uk/media-centre/press-releases/small-firms-suffer-close-to-10-000-cyber-attacks-daily (archived at https://perma.cc/Y89P-LB32)

19 Press Association (2019) Lancaster University students' data stolen in cyber-attack, *Guardian*, 23 July, www.theguardian.com/technology/2019/jul/23/lancaster-university-students-data-stolen-cyber-attack (archived at https://perma.cc/QT5F-3SHF)

20 https://www.bbc.co.uk/news/uk-england-gloucestershire-63637883 (archived at https://perma.cc/UM7G-B2NG)

21 https://www.cisa.gov/uscert/ncas/alerts/aa22-249a (archived at https://perma.cc/987Q-4NVX)

22 https://www.legalfutures.co.uk/latest-news/client-losses-from-cyber-attacks-on-law-firms-continue-to-fall (archived at https://perma.cc/U2PC-YHRH)

23 https://www.legalfutures.co.uk/latest-news/client-losses-from-cyber-attacks-on-law-firms-continue-to-fall (archived at https://perma.cc/J5AY-LRNU)

CHAPTER TWELVE

Cyber security at the board level

Cyber security issues pose key risks to organizations and should be addressed at the board level like any other business risk. In a modern business, most organizational risks will have a cyber security element to them; all board members should, therefore, have some knowledge of cyber security and recognize that good cyber security is necessary for the organization to meet its objectives. However, this is not to suggest that they should be expected to be cyber security experts. For board members, it is actually more about knowing what questions to ask and how to interpret the answers.

Cyber security is a relatively new field so it's quite natural that board members often need to develop their comfort levels with it. Cyber security has also been – and is still too often – seen as a technical domain, which has stunted the extent to which organizations have adequately engaged with it at the human and business level. It is important that cyber risks are elevated from their technical detail to be captured, and managed, in business terms, which is why it is so critical for organizations to have board members with a level of understanding in cyber security within a business context. It is crucial that board members without experience and knowledge of cyber security develop their understanding to such an extent that they are able to engage in agreeing on and monitoring their organization's cyber risk approach, and they are comfortable enough with the domain to be able to ask pertinent questions (and be able to interpret the answers!). This chapter is intended to support board members who want to develop their cyber security understanding, as well as provide a steer for those with ambitions to reach the board at a future stage. Likewise, if you are a cyber security professional who is going to be working with the board, this chapter will give you an overview of their role and responsibilities and help you understand how you can frame discussions of cyber security in a way that will be more relevant to them.

Cyber security frameworks

Cyber security frameworks can help everyone in an organization agree about the approach that the organization is taking to cyber security – and why. Working with a cyber security framework can help organizations manage the complexities of regulatory environments, and put a structure in place to make cyber security more manageable. Adopting a cyber security framework also enables organizations to demonstrate to clients, customers and other stakeholders a commitment towards cyber security; in fact, some customers require their suppliers to adhere to particular cyber security standards. The most common cyber security frameworks include the National Institute of Standards and Technology Cybersecurity Framework, ISO 27001 and Cyber Essentials. Which framework an organization adopts, and how they adopt it, will differ according to the organization itself, but for many cyber security leaders the adoption of a framework is a fundamental foundation of a strong cyber security regime.

Cyber security governance

Cyber security governance is concerned with how an organization manages its cyber security risk: how cyber security activities are structured and coordinated. At its most fundamental, cyber security governance is about ensuring that a framework of accountability and responsibility is in place in an organization. This means *what* cyber security decisions need to be made, *who* will make them, *how* they will make them, *when* they will make those decisions and, above this, *who* will oversee this structure; the checks and balances that will be in place to ensure that everything is working as well as possible.

Cyber security governance regimes differ according to the size, sector, culture and budget of the organization as well as its external environment, for example its customer base, and legal and regulatory requirements. Like all elements of cyber security risk management, having a successful governance structure framework is about knowing your organization: the risks you operate with and appetite limitations of those risks, the information that is most critical to your business (and would be most sought-after by adversaries) and the culture of your organization. The true test of a cyber security governance structure is how well it works in operation; for example, whether there is clarity of responsibilities at all levels of the organization, whether people are empowered to appropriately manage risks within these levels of responsibility and the extent to which this structure enables the organization to operate in a way that facilitates security at the same time as operational success. It is fundamental that cyber security governance structures work in harmony with other frameworks, for example data privacy and protection frameworks, to avoid contradictions, gaps or overlaps while maintaining responsibility and accountability.

In terms of cyber security governance at the board level, every board member should have a level of awareness and understanding that enables them to contribute to the organization's cyber security direction and accountability. This may manifest in different ways; for example, with some board members who are more au fait with technical elements of security, others who are more attuned to the legal dimensions and those who are more in touch with the human and cultural elements. This diversity is, of course, positive and should be encouraged; it is reflective of the fact that cyber security issues cut across many business issues and diversity of thought and experience brings new questions and solutions to the fore.

Risk appetite and risk tolerance

All organizations take risks; setting risk appetite and determining the level of risk tolerance at the board level ensures that risk-taking is considered ahead of time and made at a strategic, organization-wide level. Risk appetite can be understood as the amount and type of risk an organization is willing to accept in pursuit of its strategic business objectives; risk tolerance can be understood as the maximum risk an organization is willing to accept for each particular risk.[1] This will differ massively from organization to organization, depending on factors such as sector, size, culture and objectives, and it will change over time, as an organization grows, changes direction or changes leadership, and as the threat landscape morphs.

As part of risk management, board members should oversee checks and balances within their organization to ensure that the determined risk tolerance is not being exceeded (or, conversely, that the organization is not acting too risk averse and limiting the achievements of its strategic objectives). Risk management is a requirement for many organizations as part of the legal and regulatory framework they operate in, or their customers' demands. Whether a legal and regulatory requirement or not, setting risk appetite and tolerance at the organizational level enables organizations to operate with risk consciously, enabling people throughout the business to make more informed decisions. Despite the importance of an organization determining its level of risk appetite, in a UK Government study only 60 per cent of FTSE 350 businesses reported that their risk appetite is agreed and written down.[2]

Risk appetite and risk tolerance are complicated, and so making these as concrete as possible will be helpful. It is important to make risk management as measurable as possible so that it is grounded in quantifiable factors that can be tracked to identify progress (or lack of progress). This is challenging when it comes to cyber security, because there is not an agreed standard approach to quantifying cyber risk in the same way as, for example, financial risk. This is especially the case when it comes to human-based risk and issues such as cyber security culture. For the best part of the last decade, I've been helping organizations to measure and improve their cyber security cultures, but for many people the myth still persists that the human side of cyber security is too intangible to be quantified. The human side of cyber security can be measured just as accurately as the technical side, and doing so is just as vital: when organizations fail to measure and monitor their progress in cyber security culture, awareness and behaviours, they often fail to give these crucial elements of security the attention – and budget – that they require.

The board perspective on cyber security

How organizations *should* manage cyber security and how they *do* often differs. To identify how cyber security is being governed in practice in some of the most successful businesses, the UK Government releases a report every year that details how FTSE 350 companies approach cyber risk governance.

In 2022, the report found that:

- 82 per cent of boards or senior management within UK businesses rate cyber security as a 'very high' or 'fairly high' priority, an increase on 77 per cent in 2021.
- 50 per cent of businesses and 42 per cent of charities say they update the board on cyber security matters at least quarterly.

However, the analysis highlighted some concerns, referring to 'a number of challenges about how to translate board engagement with cyber security into increased cyber resilience amongst businesses'. Despite board engagement, especially in larger companies, the lack of cyber security expertise among board members was found to be a challenge to convincing senior leadership of the seriousness of cyber security threats and represented a barrier to securing funding.[3]

These findings highlight common contradictions we see at play in cyber security: organizations will state that they recognize the importance of cyber security but not provide dedicated funds to ensure cyber security measures are actively taken; they will put plans in place but not bring those plans to life by testing them. Having an incident response plan in place is good, for example, but without testing the workings of the plan and how details function in practice, there is a high likelihood that some issues will not have been considered and there will be gaps in the processes when they are used. If the first time these details are tested is when responding to a real, active incident, the response will of course not be as comprehensive or helpful as it could have been. Testing the plans ahead of time helps to ensure that people and processes are as resilient as possible when they are most needed.

Some of the contradictions highlighted by the UK Government report can only be tackled at the board level, for example the level of understanding that board members have of cyber security. Other issues can be positively influenced by board members providing challenge to those who are responsible for enacting cyber security within the organization on a day-to-day basis, for example the testing of incident response plans. One of the key roles of board members is to provide challenge to their organization as a way of pushing it forwards.

Board members as challengers

Board members are there to represent the stakeholders of an organization and make sure that a company is as prosperous as possible, meeting its strategic objectives in a way that is sustainable and resilient. This means protecting the interests of the organization, and it requires board members to provide appropriate levels of challenge to safeguard the organization's interests.

The UK National Cyber Security Centre (NCSC) lists key questions for the board to ask to facilitate productive, strategic conversations between board members and the organization's technical team (these questions would facilitate conversations between the board and the operational teams in general, not just the technical teams). In terms of cyber security risk, these questions are:

1 As an organization, do we have a process that ensures decision makers are as well informed as possible?
2 As an organization, do we have a process that ensures cyber risk is integrated with business risk?
3 As an organization, do we have an effective and appropriate approach to manage cyber risk?
4 As a board, have we clearly set out what types of risks we would be willing to accept?[4]

The NCSC published these questions to support board members to identify what 'good' looks like in terms of cyber security risk in their organization. With these questions, the NCSC is encouraging board members to reflect on cyber security and whether they, as board members, have enough expertise to understand the nuances of cyber security as it relates to their organization, who oversees cyber security at the organizational level and how responsibility for cyber security is integrated with the functioning of the board.

This last point is worth expanding, as many organizations approach organizational cyber security reporting lines differently. Some organizations will have a chief information security officer (CISO) who reports directly to the board, some will have a CISO who reports directly to the chief executive officer (CEO) and others will have a CISO that reports to a chief information officer (CIO) who, in turn, reports to the board. In 2020, ClubCISO found that 53 per cent of CISOs (the majority) reported to a CIO (or Chief Technology Officer, CTO) but only 16 per cent thought this was where they should report; 35 per cent thought they should report to the main board, but only 20 per cent actually did.[5] This highlights a dichotomy between where CISOs function within their organization and where they believe they would more effectively function. It seems that many CISOs feel restricted when they do not have a direct line to the board.

The NCSC questions are extremely helpful in encouraging board members to reflect on cyber security in their organization and in helping shape discussions at the board level, and between the board level and those who are managing cyber security on a day-to-day basis. The questions are also helpful because they are not overwhelming and they enable board members to start a practical, strategic discussion about a topic that is vast and that can become entrenched in technicalities.

I would encourage board members to seek out information on how well prepared their organization is to respond to a material cyber attack or data breach. As a board member, I would be keen to explore whether the organization runs scenario-based exercises (and I would want to be involved in some) and I would be keen to understand how the whole organization is prepared for the possibility of being involved in an incident. I would phrase the initial question along the lines of:

As an organization, how are we prepared for responding to a material cyber incident?

I use the word 'material' because many cyber incidents can occur in an organization that do not need a large response or the involvement of the board. However, when an incident is large and has an organizational impact that may be financial, reputational, customer-related (for example, the loss of customer data), hamper the ability of people within the organization to do their job – or all of the above – that would be a material incident.

I would also encourage board members to investigate how the different dimensions of cyber security are managed in their organization, namely the human, physical and technical elements. If board members, for example, find that most reporting on cyber issues focuses on technology, I would expect them to ask a question such as:

As an organization, how are we addressing the interplay of human, physical and technical issues in our cyber security?

With a question such as this, I would encourage board members to seek to draw out information that acknowledges the different elements of cyber security at an organizational level. I would expect a cyber security strategy that encompasses the holistic nature of cyber security. I would be keen to understand the cultural and awareness-raising plans of the organization, including whether culture is measured and metrics are in place to track the development of the cyber security culture. As a board member, I would also want to know how physical security is addressed at an organizational level and, if it is managed separately to cyber security, whether that management is siloed or working in harmony.

Last but far from least, I would want to receive ongoing communication on the threats that the organization is actively managing: what breaches have the cyber security team had to deal with, how were lessons learned from these, and what are the most pressing vulnerabilities relevant to the organization as it stands? For example, a highly visible leadership team may mean that the organization is receiving a lot of CEO fraud emails, a new technical vulnerability may mean that a crucial patch is being applied throughout the organization and a boost in financial success, such as extra investment or elevation to the FTSE 350, could have raised the profile of the organization to such an extent that the threat landscape has widened significantly in all areas. I would be keen to understand how we, as an organization, are kept up to date with all changes in the threat landscape and what threat intelligence measures we have in place. If the organization has not (yet) had to deal with a cyber incident, as a board member I would want to know whether this was because we had a very robust security regime in place, whether we had poor detection and reporting that may have missed incidents or whether we had simply been lucky so far.

Cyber security as a business risk

At the start of this chapter, I mentioned that cyber security should be addressed at the board level just like any other business risk. Whilst that is the case, it comes with some nuance. The newness of cyber security means that even board members who have some experience of it are unlikely to be as attuned to dealing with cyber issues in the same way as financial risks. Cyber security is also incredibly broad, not just covering technical, human and physical domains, but also a vast variety of in-depth specialisms within those domains. It is challenging for cyber security professionals to maintain a broad level of understanding of the whole set of subjects, and the diversity of the field can prompt imposter syndrome in even the most experienced cyber security professional, so it is certainly a challenge for non-experts to get to grips with. It is most important for board members to have a good general overview of the field, to understand cyber risks as they relate to their organization and to keep some tabs on cyber attacks and issues as they occur in peer organizations. On top of this, feeling confident in how cyber security is being managed throughout the organization, and that the culture of cyber security is strong and positive, are of course vital.

Knowing which questions to ask, how and when to ask them, is the most important skill of a board member. The newness of the field means that accepted knowledge can change very rapidly in cyber security, probably quicker than in any other part of a business. New risks emerge, technology evolves and our understanding of some core concepts of the domain shift over time. Security professionals, like anyone, can become stuck in their ways of thinking and so board members can provide an avenue for challenging the logic of security approaches in an organization. Let's take the human side of security as an example. For many years, decades even, it was widely accepted in security that users should be regarded as the weakest link. This perspective of course influenced how people within an organization were regarded by their security team and the approach that was taken regarding policies, procedures, training and technology made available to end-users. Awareness-raising training, for example, would often refer to people as the problem. So, as an end-user, you are sitting through training which tells you that you are the weakest link in your organization! I can think of little else that would be as demoralizing, uninspiring and off-putting. Thankfully, the rest of the security world has started to catch up and recognize that it is not acceptable or effective to talk about people in this way. Insights from psychology, sociology, behavioural economics and more have started to convince some professionals in the field who had been less focused on the human dimension of security to shift their narrative. However, there are still many, many security professionals out there who have not kept pace with this change and shifted their understanding or their narrative. This is one way that board members can bring an outside perspective. If the culture of their organization sees people as the problem, it doesn't take a board member having cyber security knowledge to challenge that, it simply takes experience of working with people and (so-called) common sense.

Cloud computing is another good example. Up until a few years ago, it was widely accepted by the cyber security community that 'the cloud is just someone else's computer' and should not be trusted. On-premises (on-prem) storage solutions were generally accepted as much more preferable. This has changed immensely in the last few years, with technology providers responding to security concerns and providing more robust security, more transparency and more options based on security and privacy needs (the ability to determine in which geographical jurisdictions your data is stored, for example). This, combined with the business benefits of the cloud (including the ability to embrace machine learning at a much greater scale, the ability to back-up data more effectively and the cost-saving opportunities), means that the cloud now proves to be a better business choice for many organizations than on-prem storage. Due to the rapidity with which this change has happened, many security professionals are still unaware of the shift in the cloud and, for many, the cloud is still seen as inherently insecure. This is why it is so important to ensure, as a board member, that your security team are open-minded, keep up to date with the changing landscape of security (for example through attending conferences and undertaking training) and that you provide an informed level of challenge to the security approach of your organization.

Notes

1   Ernst & Young (2010) *Risk Appetite: The strategic balancing act*, Ernst & Young

2   HM Government (2019) *FTSE 350 Cyber Risk Governance: Health check 2018*, https://assets.publishing.service.gov.uk/government/uploads/system/uploads/attachment_data/file/798068/FTSE_350_Cyber_Governance_Health_Check_2018_-_main_report.pdf (archived at https://perma.cc/FAL7-VEHK)

3   https://www.gov.uk/government/statistics/cyber-security-breaches-survey-2022/cyber-security-breaches-survey-2022#chapter-3-awareness-and-attitudes (archived at https://perma.cc/A6LD-YYQQ)

4   National Cyber Security Centre (2019) Cyber Security Toolkit for Boards, www.ncsc.gov.uk/collection/board-toolkit (archived at https://perma.cc/5BJ3-KKEE)

5   ClubCISO (2020) Information Security Maturity Report 2020: Full survey results: www.clubciso.org/downloads (archived at https://perma.cc/G2KM-MTSP)

CHAPTER THIRTEEN

Pursuing a cyber security career

Two questions I am commonly asked are 'How did you get started in cyber security?' and 'How can I get started in cyber security?' I was very lucky to find myself working in this industry and I consider it a huge blessing that I found something I am hugely passionate about. It was not a career I had even considered – I was barely aware of it – until I was headhunted by a start-up consultancy. On top of that, the little I knew about the industry gave me the impression that it was an exclusively technical discipline, and this did not seem accessible to me. And my story isn't that uncommon; many people of my age and stage in cyber security stumbled into it. Cyber security was not taught when I was at school – we were only in the early stages of having the internet – nor when I was at university.

Since I started in the sector, I have seen cyber security being taught in schools; university degrees in subjects such as ethical hacking and cyber psychology; and many great initiatives set up to develop people's skills in cyber security and raise awareness of careers in the industry. However, this does not mean that pathways into a cyber security career are clearly defined. There are lots of ways into a cyber security job, but no *one* way. This has many benefits, but can feel overwhelming if you're looking to get a foot in the door.

Qualifications and certifications

In the UK, there are now many universities offering cyber security degrees. The National Cyber Security Centre has granted 19 universities the status of Academic Centres of Excellence; if you're keen to get a degree, looking at these would be a great place to start. There are also many certifications you can take to gain recognition for your cyber security knowledge and skills. At the beginner level, these include: CompTIA Security+; and the EC-Council's Certified Ethical Hacker (CEH). As your career progresses, certifications for more experienced professionals include: (ISC)2's Certified Information Systems Security Professional (CISSP); and Offensive Security Certified Professional (OSCP).

Let's have a look at a few of these in a little more detail.

Security+

The aim of Security+ is to equip someone with a foundational understanding of risk management, cryptography and security vulnerabilities. Emphasizing practical skills and knowledge, passing Security+ requires demonstrating an understanding of:

- vulnerabilities, attacks and threats;
- identity and access management;
- network architecture;
- cryptography;
- risk management.

The Security+ certification covers the junior IT auditor/penetration tester job role, systems administrator, network administrator, and security administrator.

There is more information on CompTIA's website: www.comptia.org

Certified Ethical Hacker

CEH was designed to equip individuals with an ethical hacking methodology to be used in penetration testing. It is aimed at security professionals and anyone interested in understanding the integrity of network infrastructure and penetration testing. The certification covers scanning networks, vulnerability analysis, malware threats, social engineering, cryptography and much more.

To undertake the CEH exam, an individual must have at least two years' experience in information security, or they must complete official EC-Council training.

Find out more about CEH via EC-Council's website: www.eccouncil.org

Certified Information Systems Security Professional

CISSP is aimed at experienced security professionals who can demonstrate that they can design, implement and manage a security programme at the organizational level. The CISSP exam evaluates across eight areas of security:

- security and risk management;
- asset security;
- security architecture and engineering;
- communication and network security;
- identity and access management;
- security assessment and testing;
- security operations;
- software development security.

To qualify for the certification, an individual must have at least five years of cumulative, paid work experience in two or more of the eight domains above. It is aimed at people in positions such as security manager, security analyst, IT manager, director of security and chief information security officer.

Find out more about CISSP via (ISC)2's website: www.isc2. org

Offensive Security Certified Professional

OSCP is an advanced certification focused on penetration testing. Those taking the certification are expected to have a good understanding of TCP/IP networking, a fair understanding of Linux, and are advised that familiarity with Bash scripting with basic Python or Perl would be beneficial. The certification is aimed at penetration testers, security professionals and network administrators. The OSCP is a 24-hour lab-based exam with a written element, aimed at testing an individual's time management skills as well as their technical expertise. Passing the exam involves exploiting machines in the lab, documenting your work and submitting a final report.

There is more information on Offensive Security's website: www.offensive-security.com

University study

Given that I took an academic route up to and including PhD level, it would be remiss of me not to mention the benefits of university study. Completing a degree teaches you not only about the subject of study, but also equips you with transferable skills that include time management, written and oral communication skills, how to conduct research, team working experience, self-study discipline and more. If you want to pursue a cyber security career, undertaking a degree in the subject would give you a chance to learn some of the foundational subjects, explore the discipline and perhaps uncover those particular areas that interest you the most, demonstrate your interest in the field and make valuable contacts. There are benefits to going to university and benefits to focusing your studies on cyber security.

'Real world' experience

However, there are also benefits to *not* going to university, not least that you can potentially start working in the field sooner, gaining experience and contacts and getting 'real world' insight into what it means to work in cyber security. My university studies did not include cyber security and that is true for all professionals of my generation (unless they went to university recently); the degrees were not there to be studied and so we learned in different ways, on the job and with self-study. Whether you go to university or not, whether you study (or have studied) cyber security or not – these are personal choices that come down very much to individual circumstances and preferences.

What do employers want?

For many of us running companies and hiring individuals, we are not looking for a specific degree, qualification or certification. Of course, if it is something you are motivated and inspired to do then that's great, and hopefully you'll have seen some of the benefits outlined in the sections above; but if someone tells you that you need a piece of paper to work in cyber security, they are the wrong person to be speaking to. There are many of us working in cyber security who believe that personal attributes are most important when it comes to working in this field. Some of the most important attributes include:

• *Your ethical and moral code*: Working in cyber security, you are often in a position of trust and so it is important that those working in the industry have a strong professional set of ethics. We are often exposed to confidential, personal and sensitive information and it is imperative that we treat that with respect and afford it the privacy and security necessary. Cyber security professionals operate in highly trusted roles, seeing where organizations and individuals are vulnerable, and so you need to be trusted not to take advantage. For example, an ethical hacker performing a penetration test on a banking website may discover a vulnerability that could, technically, allow them to siphon off some money; this individual cannot profit from that discovery outside of their legal contract.

- *Curiosity*: It is often the case that the best way to identify a vulnerability is to be curious. This spans across all areas of cyber security, from technical ('I wonder what happens when I type this code there?') to physical ('This CCTV camera looks a bit off. Does it actually cover the safe door?') to human ('No one is using the right procedure to email confidential information. I wonder if it's too complicated or we haven't communicated it as well as we could?'). Being curious about the way things work, or don't work, is a great personality trait for a cyber security professional.

- *A desire to learn*: This does not have to be learning in any kind of formal way (I don't mean you need to love textbooks!), but as the field of cyber security is constantly shifting with new technology, new vulnerabilities and new forms of attack and defence, it is beneficial if you enjoy staying informed and, even more so, if you have a knack for putting together information from different places or disciplines.

- *An acceptance that you don't know everything* (and that's ok): At the same time as having a desire to learn and drive to acquire more knowledge, you will benefit from acknowledging that you don't have all the answers when it comes to security, that it is a very wide field and people from different areas of security will have knowledge that can inform and enhance your understanding. An open mind is *crucial* in cyber security, so that you can see problems from other people's points of view and consider solutions that might not have been immediately obvious to you. It is easy to get overwhelmed in security and to believe that everyone else knows more than you and you never know enough, because the field is so wide and fast-paced. At the other end of the scale, there is a danger that people become entrenched in their own narrow area of expertise and over-estimate their value compared to other people. Develop resilience in the face of this: seek more knowledge and refine your skills but stay open-minded to learn from other perspectives. Resist the Dunning-Kruger effect, the cognitive bias in which people over-estimate their intelligence to be higher than it actually is. Cyber security is a multi-faceted problem, which requires input from different people and areas of expertise.

- *Empathy*: Cyber security is about listening and understanding, putting yourself into someone else's shoes. For example, this can be listening to people in a business to understand what their most valuable information is, how they work and why some security rules might be really difficult for them to follow. It might also be listening to people about their personal cyber security and understanding that the 'perfect' technical solution is not going to work for them, and that you need to find them a solution they will actually engage with. As a cyber security professional, I would love it if everyone would use a password manager, but I need to understand that they might not be accessible enough for some people.

These personality traits can all be developed, and demonstrating them will be appealing to prospective employers. There are other skills you can hone, too:

- *Situational awareness*: This is a baseline for anyone wanting to enhance their level of security. Situational awareness often comes down to observational skills, having an understanding of what is happening around you and the potential impact of that. Ask yourself questions such as: Has my company identity pass been swiped from my bag? Am I speaking about confidential information in a public place? Is someone tailgating behind me when I enter the office?

- *Spotting patterns*: As a cyber security professional, you will often have to identify what 'bad' or 'unusual' looks like, which means knowing what 'good' or 'normal' looks like. Noticing patterns is a skill that benefits those working in offensive security (for example, if you are going to simulate an attack on an organization, being able to spot some abnormal code or a break in their physical perimeter is going to be crucial to your success) and those working in defensive security (for example, if you are analysing internet traffic coming into an organization's network, identifying unusual traffic is a must).

- *Communication skills*: Whatever role you have in cyber security, it is likely that you will need a level of communication skills. This will vary from the skills needed to communicate well with your team members about the project you are working on, needing to explain technical issues in a report that is going to people that don't have the same level of technical knowledge as you, to needing to explain to colleagues why some security rules are important and not just there to be a blocker or something they seek to work around.

What can you do to get a job in the industry?

This really depends on your personal circumstances. If you are at school or university, see if there is a cyber or hacking club or society that you can join. If not, set one up! Look into some of the amazing initiatives for young people that may be available to you.

If you are already in the workplace and there is a cyber security or information security team in your organization, why not approach them and see if you could learn more about what they do? You may find that there is a champion or ambassador programme in your organization, in which people in non-security roles volunteer to represent security in their department, in the same way that we have health and safety representatives or fire wardens. If so, these initiatives are often great ways to increase your understanding of the field, get some experience and training and boost your CV.

There are many cyber security community conferences, events and meet-ups happening all around the world, and these are often free or low-cost to attend.

DEFCON groups

DEFCON groups (DCGs) grew out of the annual DEFCON conference in Las Vegas, which began in 1993 as a place for people interested in hacking to meet. As stated on the DEFCON website:

> DCG meetings are open to anyone, regardless of their skill, age, job, gender, etc. DCGs are designed to help you learn new things, meet new people, mentor others in areas you may be strong in, and provide some cohesion within the hacker culture and its members.[1]

At the time of writing, there are 270 DCGs worldwide, covering half of the United States and in over 20 countries around the world, from Algeria to Zimbabwe. DCGs are usually informal, local, monthly meet-ups where you can meet people interested in hacking and cyber security and perhaps listen to a talk or take part in a workshop. They are often a great place to get to know people in your local security community, so it is worth discovering if there is a group near you, or, if there is not, consider setting up your own. There is more information on the DEFCON Groups website: https://defcongroups.org

BSides

BSides are security community events, aimed at enabling people in the community to meet, present their ideas and research and listen to others sharing their knowledge. BSides are run by local community teams and so they vary, but they are most often an annual conference with a call for presentations (CFP) in advance of the event, to which people can submit a topic they would like to speak about, which is then voted on by the community. Many BSides also run rookie tracks, in which people new to the industry or new to speaking can present in a smaller room with the support of a mentor, as well as lightning tracks, which offer shorter speaking slots that you sign up for on the day of the event.

JACK DANIEL, BSIDES CO-FOUNDER

I'm a displaced mechanic who landed in automotive management where I had to learn to work with computers and soon took over computer operations and administration. If you did systems and network admin in the 1990s, you learned about security whether you wanted to or not. I liked it and gradually shifted focus to security. As I was thrown into tech, I discovered local user groups and learned much from them. When I had something to share, I shared it – that started my long involvement in community engagement. When I saw the US auto industry decline on the horizon, I joined the vendor side, first at Astaro, and later at Tenable, where I have been for over eight years. Both companies have been incredibly supportive of my community engagement work.

In 2009 many in the hacker and security communities had come together on Twitter, and when people started discussing the talks that were turned down at the bigger conferences a few of us looked and saw some interesting ideas so we made a place for people to share their presentations and discussions. Although there had been some discussions on how to make conferences better, we didn't intend to create a series, and certainly never expected to launch a global movement, but people wanted more, and the BSides idea took off. As we discussed the keys to BSides' success and growth, we found four core ideas, each building on the others. First was content – interesting ideas are shared.

Second was conversation – since the events are smaller and more informal, the presentations are usually more conversational, ideas are shared and discussed. Third is community – if you share ideas and spark conversation, people build and strengthen the local (and often global) hacker and infosec communities. Last, but not least, is career – if you share and discuss ideas in a healthy and growing community, people will naturally progress in their careers as they see what topics are hot, what companies are hiring and who has what expertise.

Capture the flags

'Capture the flags' competitions often run at events and conferences like BSides, and they also run online. They usually run within a set timeframe and consist of a series of challenges that participants solve using different skills, and when you complete a challenge, you are awarded a flag and earn points. People complete capture the flags (CTFs) on their own or in teams. The more you take part in CTFs, the more you learn how they work and what you can do to maximize points.

CTFs generally include challenges that cover lots of different skillsets, including open source intelligence, programming, cyptography, hacking, networks, forensics and more. This makes them very democratic: obviously, the more skilled you are, the more likely you are to get points, but whether you are experienced or not, or technical or not, you are likely to get a flag or two if you have a go and persevere. Working as a team can be beneficial because of the variety of challenges, but also because it enables you to practise team-working skills, become known for what you are good at and build up your connections.

SOPHIA McCALL, CAPTAIN OF TEAM UK AT THE EUROPEAN CYBER SECURITY CHALLENGE

I have always been interested in computers and technology from a young age. From as early as primary school I would excel in subjects such as IT. This continued through my secondary school years and eventually the completion of my BTEC Extended Diploma in Software Development. Originally I wanted to be a programmer, but during the completion of my BTEC at college I soon discovered that breaking things was a lot more fun than building them! And that sparked my interest in cyber security. From college I then went on to pursue a degree in cyber security management, which provided me with the essential knowledge of business management and policy decisions in a security context. In addition to this, I built up my technical skills, which then allowed me to pursue the dream job of a technical security consultancy role after university.

CTF competitions helped me grow and hone my technical skills in addition to the managerial skills I was learning from my cyber security management degree. At first, I used CTFs as a way to pursue additional security topics outside of my scheduled university hours – but it soon turned from a hobby to a passion, and I am grateful that I got involved early on in my degree. Everything technical, I originally learned from CTFs – they prove an exemplary learning tool to teach the basics of ethical hacking. As President of the Computing and Security Society at my university in my final year, I gravitated towards using CTFs to teach our members (most of whom had limited to no security experience) the fundamentals of ethical hacking and cyber security technical skills. When I first started at university, I struggled with being 'technical' – I struggled, a lot! But through perseverance and completion of an array of competitions and labs I saw myself go from 'zero to hero' – going from a novice CTFer that struggled to get a single flag, to Captain of Team UK at the European Cyber Security Challenge in a short span of two years. I can't thank the existence of such competitions enough, and I encourage anyone and everyone of all abilities to get involved when they can.

As the budding security professional I am today, I thank organizations like Cyber Security Challenge UK for providing the stepping stones for individuals like myself to enter the security industry and field. Completing their competitions and boot camps and attending their community events allowed me to expand my network, create a name for myself and exercise my security skills in a healthily competitive and fun environment. Organizations such as the Challenge provided the foundations of my career, and I am very grateful for the opportunities the Challenge provided me to create the personal brand that I have today.

Bug bounties

Many organizations run bug bounty programmes, in which they set specific guidelines to reward people who find 'bugs' (vulnerabilities) in their websites, software or applications. This enables the organization to crowd-source the finding of vulnerabilities, with the aim of increasing their chances of identifying and fixing them before they are found and exploited by cyber criminals or result in a data breach due to data leakage. There are organizations, such as Bugcrowd and HackerOne, which manage bug bounties on behalf of organizations, acting as a bridge between the organizations running bug bounties and the hackers looking for bugs.

Develop your network

In an industry based on trust, networking is important. Getting to know people, and them to know you, can really help you move ahead in your career. This doesn't have to be in person – engage in conversations on Twitter, look for some of the cyber security Discord groups to join, or set up your own blog. People sometimes worry that they don't know enough to write a blog, but you don't have to be an 'expert' to share your learnings or your passion for a subject. As long as you don't claim to have knowledge or experience that you don't possess, then blog posts can cover subjects you are just learning about, a technology that you have just started applying or a project that you completed.

There is a lot to learn when it comes to cyber security, and while you should definitely not feel that you need to know it all in great depth (that would be impossible!), it is important to develop knowledge and skills in the area you pursue (for example, that might be forensics, penetration testing, organizational cyber security culture or one of the many other areas). This will be true throughout your career, as new technology is developed and new vulnerabilities are found. There is a wealth of information out there and much of it is freely accessible. There are of course many excellent books you can read, but there are also podcasts, video tutorials, blog sites, email newsletters and much more you can engage with to learn and stay in the know.

Note

1   DEFCON Groups (2019) The latest, https://defcongroups.org (archived at https://perma.cc/KY4W-VM3F)

CHAPTER FOURTEEN

The variety of cyber security careers

I hope reading this book so far has given you a good overview of the breadth of cyber security. It is a discipline that cuts across human, technical and physical issues, with dimensions that cover legal, business and geopolitical domains, as well as much more. This chapter will introduce you to some of the many different careers in this industry, by profiling people who work in the field. I asked the amazing people featured to explain what they do, what they like about it, what their backgrounds are and what advice they would give their younger selves.

The start-up CEO

David Shipley is the CEO of Beauceron, a behaviour and culture change platform that empowers employees from the front line to senior executives on their role in cyber security.

I love how Shipley describes his job:

My job is to be the chief storyteller. I help our team, investors, customers and the public understand the story of cyber – of people in control of technology – and why they should care about it. Creating and sharing stories is the original – and still the best – way to help teach and learn. When a story resonates, people feel connected emotionally as well as cognitively to the issue or idea and you have buy-in for a shared purpose.

What I love about my job is the ability to make a difference in the world. All around me I see the consequences of our predictable human failure to prepare for the consequences of our technological revolution. Whether it's families coping with trying to protect their children from a horde of internet predators or small businesses trying to avoid losing what little money they have to ever more sophisticated fraudsters, or political actors trying to protect democracy itself from internet-fuelled hate and propaganda, the need to put people in control of technology has never been greater.

Every time we help teach employees at a business about social engineering, or we contribute to public policy debates on greater accountability for social media companies or do a media interview with advice for parents, we get wins.

The day when we reached 100 per cent completion on training a police department on cyber security was one of my proudest ever as CEO. We helped protect police so they can help protect citizens. The day we deployed our technology to one of the biggest financial institutions in North America is a close second because if we helped in educating and protecting that bank, it will help protect individuals and businesses.

Like many people working in security, Shipley has a diverse – and fascinating – background. The theme of his career is a desire to help others and be part of positive change in the world. His outlook on life, and work, is one which I find inspiring:

My advice for my younger self is to be kind to yourself, and you never know where life's journey will take you. Every step in the journey will make more sense as you get older. Also, it's okay to not have all the answers. As you get older, you'll realize it's never about the answers but rather it's about the questions you ask along the way.

Twenty years ago this summer I was a young soldier who was exposed to some of the hard truths of our world while helping care for and protect Kosovar refugees who fled violence in their homeland and sought refuge in Canada. That experience and the many, many questions that came from it prompted me to pursue higher education. When I left the military in 2003, I took that education and became a journalist.

When I left journalism in 2008 to become a marketer at a university, I thought I was taking the easy way out and wasn't helping protect or inform society as I had in the past. What I didn't realize was I was being given the opportunity to combine all of my skills with new experiences to have a greater impact on an international scale.

When I turned 40 this year, I looked back at my life to date and tried to make some sense of it. I realized that while it's felt like a series of crazy twists and turns – soldier, journalist, marketer, cyber security lead, CEO – there was a common theme: a passion for making a difference in the world and telling stories, as well as a desire to be part of something bigger than myself.

The final piece of advice I'd give my younger self is this: no man or woman achieves anything great on their own. It always takes a community to truly make lasting change happen.

There was a time, when I first went down the Alice in Wonderland rabbit-hole of cyber security in 2012, that the sheer scale and scope of the problems in cyber security felt overwhelming and disheartening. But over the last few years as we formed our company I reached a greater understanding of the growing army of much smarter women and men around the world who are in this fight for the long haul. I wasn't alone. Far from it, in fact. I could learn new things from all of them and do more good.

The infosec pundit

Like David Shipley, Carole Theriault is also driven by a passion to make positive change and help people be more secure, which she does via the digital communications agency that she founded, Tick Tock Social, and in her role as a well-known information security podcaster and writer. This is how Theriault describes herself and her work:

> Effectively I'm an infosecurity pundit with stonkingly diverse responsibilities. It all boils down to me wanting to help humans be more aware of today's state of technology and help them better fend off the bad stuff. It is not an overstatement to say it's the tech wild west out there.
>
> I am founder and CEO of Tick Tock Social Limited, a consultancy based in Oxford in the UK. Before its launch in 2013, I had spent 20 years climbing the ranks in a variety of well-respected technology and security organizations. Today, Tick Tock Social works with technology firms, nonprofits and government bodies around the world to improve infosecurity standards, strategies and communications. This ranges from creating communication strategies in an infosecurity crisis, presenting at conferences or evening shindigs, to working with institutions to set global infosecurity standards.
>
> In 2016, I co-founded Smashing Security, where I continue to co-host and produce the award-winning weekly tech podcast. It gives a fresh twist on the latest cyber SNAFUs and provides insight, giggles and advice to its army of listeners. While this started as a grassroots effort, today, Smashing Security total downloads are well into the millions, with a dedicated and passionate core audience. I also regularly contribute on other podcasts, such as The Cyberwire podcast network, hosting and producing interviews with world-leading tech experts.

One of the elements of cyber security that I love the most is how much there is to learn and the really interesting people that you get to meet as part of that learning. This field is built on sharing knowledge; most people who work in cyber security love to learn, to share what they have learnt and to soak up knowledge that others share. I've worked for myself and run my own companies for a lot of my career, and this is partly because it allows me to go on that journey of following my curiosity and seeing where the learning takes me, rather than having someone else dictate the direction that I take. This is something Theriault and I have in common:

> I love a bold challenge and meeting brainy tech lovers, and that's what I spend my days doing. I connect with people I find interesting, and then pick their brains. Working for yourself is like nothing else. Sure, it's incredibly complex and daunting at first, but once a good rhythm sets in, it's as wonderful as riding a bike on a quiet sunny day. I get involved in the projects that interest and excite me, and belly laugh on a daily basis. So ya, it's pretty sweet.

Working for yourself also allows you (if you plan for it) to build a way of working that fits your life, which means a lot to Theriault:

> Having years ago found myself too close to burnout for comfort, I try to limit work hours to 4–6 hours a day, though that sometimes means weekend days too. I juggle running the company, preparing or giving a talk, interviewing guests and producing podcasts, as well as assisting our Tick Tock Social team with clients.

I asked Theriault what advice she would give to her younger self, and these top five tips are like gold dust (they also give you a sense of her warm personality and infectious sense of humour).

Her advice will be relevant to people at all stages of their careers, but especially if you are early on in your journey:

1 You are awesome. Just do you and be the best you can be.
2 Calm down. No one expects you to know everything. When you start your career, acting like a know-it-all is an extreme red flag to those who've earned their stripes. Just pay attention, retain what you learn, and practise again and again until you know it inside out.
3 Bosses really, really matter, and they can take a toll on your mental health if it is not a good fit. This doesn't mean they are bad people. Sometimes, you just don't see eye to eye. So if you often feel stressed or anxious, or if you often feel misunderstood, know that boss is not good for you. Get out.
4 Organizations really, really matter, and if you don't agree morally or ethically with how they operate, do not even hesitate in saying no, even if there is a big, fat pay cheque.
5 A network is different from friendships, but building a good one means you have a strong work family. Start right now, whether you are at school, uni or work. Wherever you are, you will meet interesting and inspiring people. These are the people that can guide you, share experiences, find you great jobs, help you change careers... A good one is as valuable as gold. Choose them well and nurture your work family. If properly maintained, they will see you through the inevitable storms we all face from time to time.

The professor

Theriault makes so many good points with her advice, not least that when you're early on in your career, it's accepted that there will be lots you don't know, and that's nothing to be ashamed of. None of us can be expected to know everything, especially in a field as diverse as cyber security. Professor Shujun Li has some really good advice in this area:

> Cyber security is a fast-growing and increasingly interdisciplinary field, and not a technical subject only computer scientists and electronic engineers can do something with. Cyber security has also a lot of overlaps with another hot topic – AI – where we can see two important sub-areas: security of AI, and AI for security. I strongly encourage more young people to consider a future career in cyber security, or even cyber security and AI together. Due to its interdisciplinary nature, you need to try to be good at going broad as much as you can, but be prepared to transform yourself to be good at going deep if your interest is more focused on a smaller area of cyber security. Even if you want to be a specialist, you still need to have sufficient exposure to a broad range of fundamental knowledge and skills, in order to be able to better understand complicated cyber security problems in the real world. When you are out of school, it is important to keep a close eye on recent news on ICT technologies (not just cyber security) and try to do as many hands-on exercises with computer hardware and software as possible, to develop a more comprehensive understanding of the cyber security landscape.

Much like Carole Theriault, Li appreciates the freedom that his line of work allows him:

> What I enjoy the most as an academic is the freedom to do things I like and what I consider important, interesting and useful. This is something no other types of job can offer, so even though I am not as well paid as other people working in industry I still like my job. I also enjoy the endless opportunities to work with people from other disciplines, sectors and also students who are interested in conducting research.

Li is Professor of Cyber Security at the University of Kent in the UK, leading the Kent Interdisciplinary Research Centre in Cyber Security, a UK Government-recognized Academic Centre of Excellence in Cyber Security Research. Working in academia has enabled him to mould his career as he moved through it:

> I was trained more as an electronic engineer at university (back in the 1990s), although my first degree is considered a mixture of three closely related subjects: electronic engineering, computer science and automatic control. After getting my PhD degree in information and communication engineering from the Xi'an Jiaotong University in China in 2003, I first worked in electronic engineering at two universities in Hong Kong from 2003–07, and then moved to a German university where I shifted to computer science. Since then I have stayed within computer science and gradually re-labelled myself as a computer scientist. After working at two German universities for four years, I moved into the UK in 2011. Before I started working on cyber security in 1999, my research interests were mostly around image and video processing, which remains one of my current research interests.

The journalist

As we saw with David Shipley earlier, having a diverse background is the norm in cyber security. This industry has evolved very organically, alongside the organic growth of the internet. There were no cyber security courses or degrees until quite recently; those of us of a certain age and generation in the industry would never have been told about cyber security careers at school, because those careers did not exist. We have found our way and forged our careers as we move forwards, which often means an unusual career path.

For example, the journalist Kate O'Flaherty did not originally plan to focus on cyber security. O'Flaherty is a freelance journalist and copywriter, who writes content that appears in the press, such as Forbes, the *Guardian* and SC Magazine. She also writes on behalf of clients such as security companies, but this focus on cyber security was not always her plan:

> When I was younger, I wanted to be a music journalist – I couldn't have imagined going into technology, let alone cyber security. But if I could give my younger self advice, I'd tell myself to consider security and tech more generally earlier on.

Alternative paths into cyber security

Lance Spitzner, Director of SANS Security Awareness, also had a winding path into this profession, and recognizes the many advantages that his background equipped him with. Spitzner started out on the technical side: he founded the Honeynet Project and is on the Board of Directors for the US National Cyber Security Alliance. This is what he had to say about his background before this industry:

> I'm a history major who rode main battle tanks for a living. But often unique backgrounds can be an advantages in this field. For example, history taught me how to write and communicate. The military taught me about leadership and knowing your enemy.

Moussa Noun's journey into security is equally fascinating. Having worked around the world on documentary films, he is now security awareness manager at a major Canadian financial institution. He is an example of someone who is excelling in their career without having taken an academic route. As well as film making, his background includes software development, pen testing and project management, and his security mindset enabled him to absorb expertise from some unlikely places:

> From a very young age I was fascinated with convincing people to do things. I would try different sentences and different ways

of saying them, sort of looking for a 'cheat code' into people's minds. I learned about social engineering from a book and became fascinated with the idea and tried to practise it as often as I could.

In my early 20s I was introduced to a couple of people from LA that were visiting at the time, and after a few minutes of watching them at a party I noticed they had an uncommon ease with people. I quickly realized they were pickup artists, a group of men that honed their social skills and aimed to sleep with as many women as possible. I became fascinated with their process: how do they build rapport? How do they approach strangers? Within a few months I found myself in Los Angeles observing them.

I sometimes relive those experiences and not a day goes by without using the skills and methods I had learned – even though I learned these skills from people who were using them to manipulate others and take advantage of them, I now use those same skills to positively influence people into being more secure and resisting becoming victim to social engineering attacks. Getting into the mindset of an attacker can be the best way of defending yourself and others.

Clive Room is another great example of someone who took a varied path before working in this field. As Director of Pulse Conferences, Room works with a team putting together international conferences for CISOs and other senior security professionals across the globe. Before working in cyber security, he had a very different career:

> My background is as a professional actor and then a professional tour guide, before moving into marketing for a cyber security services company. My advice to my younger self is that you may well have four different careers in one lifetime, and that's a good thing.

What Room loves about working in cyber security is common for many of us, and has already been evident in what Carole

Theriault had to say: the people. International travel also has its perks:

I enjoy the international travel that comes with my job, as well as dealing with interesting people from many different aspects of the industry. I love presenting and seeing events well organized in a way that ensures that people who meet for the first time, become friends as well as colleagues.

The ethical hacker

The ethical hacker and social engineer Freakyclown, or FC (I should add he's my husband and we run the company Cygenta together), can relate to this:

What I love about my job is the variety of it all. One day I could be hacking into a website of a media company and the next flying across the globe to talk about cyber security to thousands of people, and by the end of the week I might be breaking into a bank and stealing millions of pounds (we give it all back, obviously). There is no such thing as a typical day for me and I think that's what keeps my motivation so high. I run the company with my wife and when you run your own business, 9 to 5 working is out. We work with global clients and so sometimes I can be doing a pen test at 3 am or sitting in a ditch watching a building, plotting a break-in. A pen test is very much like an MOT for a car; it's a snapshot of time and vulnerabilities. So, today I could write up a report that lists all of the known, found vulnerabilities and then tomorrow a new one could be discovered that could devastate the system. That brings a certain level of pressure to the work, but I wouldn't do anything else. Hacking is very much a cat and mouse game with the criminals and I enjoy helping people and companies be as secure as they can be from criminals.

I get to meet and work with so many interesting people and, most importantly, I help people be safer and more secure. For more than half of my life I have been breaking into places, either physically or digitally, but always legally and ethically! It's the best job in the world as far as I'm concerned.

The lawyer

The variety of work that Freakyclown mentions is a factor that keeps Jonathan Armstrong enthusiastic about his work. Armstrong is a lawyer at Cordery, focusing on compliance issues including cyber security, and this means working on lots of different problems for all sorts of clients:

> What I like most about my job is the variety. No two days are ever the same. It's also an area where there's a skills gap – many lawyers don't understand cyber security issues so there's a chance to help a wide variety of companies large and small.

The analyst

Kenneth Geers echoes this. Geers is a world-renowned cyber intelligence analyst enjoying an amazing career that includes 20 years of experience working for the United States Government (including the NSA and NCIS) and roles as an Ambassador of NATO Cooperative Cyber Defence Centre of Excellence and a Senior Fellow with the Atlantic Council. This is how he summed up his career so far:

> I have worked in signals intelligence or cyber security since 1993, with time on offence, defence and in academia. But I have always been an intelligence analyst, in the national security space, so I care less about the 'how' of computer hacking – and more about the 'who' and the 'why'.

When I spoke to him about what he most loves about his work, he perfectly captured the diversity of cyber security as a field. Working at the international level, covering issues relating to nation-state-level cyber security, Geers highlighted the fact that cyber security is at the heart of every international issue you can think of:

> There are endless areas of research, from elections to electricity, and cryptocurrency to human rights. There were many sceptics who doubted the connection between network security and national security, but today it is clear that computer hacking (and IT-enabled social engineering) has transformed everything, including politics, crime, terrorism and war.

The national cyber security advisor

A theme that unites all of the professionals featured in this chapter is how important it is to them that their work helps keep people safe and secure. This mission is at the heart of what drives Emma W,[1] who also works at the national level of cyber security, in this case for the UK National Cyber Security Centre (NCSC):

> I'm the Head of Advice and Guidance for the NCSC. I'm in charge of making sure that the NCSC has all the right technical advice and guidance on our website, for all our different audiences, from individuals and families who are looking for short, sensible advice on how to stay safe online at home, through to security professionals who are responsible for protecting the UK's critical national infrastructure from nation-state-level cyber attacks. It's a big job and, as you can imagine, it's always a work in progress!
>
> In myself, I'm mainly about the human side of cyber security. I think cyber security should work better for people who aren't experts at it, without us all having to go and get computer science degrees first. When we're at home, we should all be able to confidently protect ourselves and our loved ones from the most

common online threats and scams. When we're at work, we are our organization's first and most important line of defence against cyber attacks – which means we need security tools, policies, processes and cultures that match people's real capabilities, and how we need to work. For too many of us, security still seems expensive, inconvenient, impenetrably technical, and generally bothersome. And we need to fix that. I generally win fans when I say 'I'm trying to help you stay safe online without having to remember a million passwords'!

More than anything, I love our mission. We're here to make the UK the world's safest place to live and work online. I can't imagine many things I could do with my life that could be more worthwhile than that. Also, we have a fantastic, diverse team at NCSC. I find it really stimulating to work in an environment where others have very different backgrounds to me, and many different skills, experiences and perspectives. We trust each other, we respect everyone's specialist knowledge, we have great discussions, and together we achieve things that none of us could do alone. Also the cake. We have a *lot* of good cake. If I were a hostile intelligence agency trying to disrupt GCHQ and NCSC, the first thing I'd target would be the cake.

Whilst of course appreciating the cake (which does sound like a very nice perk), Emma W is driven by contributing to the security of the UK at a national level, which is an amazing mission. When she talks about what her work is like on a day-to-day basis, it is clear that she is also motivated by helping those around her and by inspiring and supporting the next generation of cyber security professionals:

On a typical day, I'll be in one of our Cheltenham offices working in the awesome NCSC comms team. I'll review guidance in progress – maybe nudge something along if it's ground to a halt, or settle a debate about exactly what we should say, how and to

THE VARIETY OF CYBER SECURITY CAREERS

whom. I may meet an NCSCer who wants to produce some new guidance, to find out more about what they want to do. Who needs to hear this advice? What do they need? How are we going to do it? How important or urgent is this, compared to everything else?

I also provide specialist sociotechnical expertise to colleagues in comms, across everything we do – so I answer questions from 'Can we tell the CyberUK contractors that the event website must be hosted in the UK?' to 'How should we reply to this member of the public who's got in touch to ask for password advice, as he's been using the same password everywhere since 1994?'

That's a *typical* day, but my *favourite* days at work are either a) when I'm presenting to an audience, as I love sharing my thinking about cyber security, helping to build consensus for change, and hearing from others in return; or b) if I have someone shadowing me at work. I really enjoy giving them an insight into the things we do (there tends to be quite a few 'wows', because we do get up to some truly impressive stuff), and helping them to make useful contacts to follow up on things that interest them. Combining both those favourite things: I love it when I'm allowed out to talk to younger people about careers in cyber security. It's really important to take that time, to help grow and inspire the security professionals of the future. Many people don't realize what a diverse profession it is, and think it's not for them unless they're studying computing or maths. This is totally untrue!

When I asked Emma W about the advice she would give a younger version of herself, she perfectly summed up the feeling so many of us have in the field, that we found our way into this career without a clear path ahead of us and, perhaps connected to that, that along that path it can feel overwhelming just how big cyber security is. Working on the human side of cyber security, Emma W also touched on a reticence that many of us with this specialism can have, especially early on in our careers:

The advice I would give myself: don't worry that you don't yet know what you want to do when you grow up. Your career path will be entirely unplanned and more than a little random, but every job you do will make you better at the job after that. Cyber security needs its deep specialists, but it also needs people who are good at seeing the big picture, bringing people together from across different teams and working cultures to solve a shared problem, figuring out what needs doing and then actually getting it done, seeing where techniques that work in one domain can be usefully applied in another, and devising pragmatic, workable solutions to knotty issues. That's you.

Also, don't worry that you 'aren't technical enough' for cyber security. It won't hold you back. Cyber security really needs more 'people people' – those who understand a bit more about what makes people tick, and can represent their needs and advocate for their points of view, to help make security that works for people. Because, as we all know, security that doesn't work for people doesn't work.

I love Emma W's message above and the final line is simply perfect; I often quote this message from Emma W and the NCSC when I am delivering a conference keynote.

The security awareness leader

Lance Spitzner specializes, like Emma W and like me, in the human side of cyber security and he points out that now is a fantastic time for security awareness and culture professionals:

My speciality is the human side of security, often called security awareness or security culture. My job is to help organizations better understand and manage the human side of their cyber risks. It's an extremely exciting time to be in this field as organizations are just now recognizing that cyber security is not just a technical challenge but also a human challenge.

I love the combination of technology and the human side. I have to leverage my technical skills, and help organizations better understand their culture and build on that through engagement and partnerships. Ultimately it's all about helping people (and organizations) be more secure.

SPECIALISTS AND GENERALISTS

Spitzner's comment about combining technology with the human side echoes Emma W's earlier point about cyber security having deep specialists but also those who are good at seeing the big picture, too. When taking the messages of security and communicating them to the wider world, this is especially important; this is relevant to the NCSC, of course, and also to those working in journalism. Here's what Kate O'Flaherty had to say on this topic:

Although you need to know your area, it's ok to rely on the expertise of others: journalists are not experts, the people they speak to are. Do not be afraid to look stupid and always ask questions – people are more than happy to help.

This message will be especially pertinent to journalists, but we can all learn from O'Flaherty's advice. I am a firm believer in the message that there are no stupid questions. The only way we can evolve is to ask questions and learn, which is true both at the individual and group level. If we are working in cyber security as part of a desire to make people more secure, we have a responsibility to ask questions, because if we don't understand something, we may be limiting our ability to contribute to resolving a problem. If we want to make the world a safer place, we need to know when to swallow our pride.

The security contractor

I asked John Carroll, a security contractor, what advice he would give to his younger self, and he had some interesting thoughts on the matter:

Drink more water.

Think about your posture.

Sleep when you're tired.

It's OK to eat coco pops from a pan if the bowl isn't big enough.

Some people want your advice, some people need to look like they want your advice, you can't control that, but you can always give good advice.

And finally… you're going to be fine. This industry is constantly growing in more granular specialisms; you can try and collect them all, but make sure you have the fundamentals down. Learn how to see everything, then learn how to modify everything.

Carroll makes so many important points here (that coco pops advice is a true life lesson). Physical health is something we can all overlook when we are busy with work that we are passionate about and a lot of jobs in cyber security inherently involve long hours at a computer. Getting enough rest, staying hydrated and working on your core strength and posture may not sound like cyber security advice, but most professionals working in this field will tell you that taking care of these things from the start of your career will be an investment you are grateful for the longer you work in the industry.

Carroll's career is really interesting because of the diversity of roles he has experienced. When I asked him to describe his work and what he enjoys about it, this is what he had to say:

I would say, in short, security support: What's the problem? What additional concerns are attached? What resources do we have?

Easy...! To qualify this, over the past five years I've worked in roles such as vulnerability manager, pen test manager, head of infosec, vCISO,[2] and plenty of app security and enterprise security challenges. In between, I get to do this kind of work because I'm happy to look at problems as challenges that I can overcome in a meaningful way... so far so good... mostly!

I like thinking about things that might not yet have been considered. I like demonstrating flaws, not so much for the flaw at face value, but more what process would prevent this flaw at scale. I like being embraced by teams, and I like showing why security should be embraced by teams that might not see the need initially.

What an amazing response! Carroll's mindset shows why he is so successful in cyber security, because he sees problems as challenges waiting to be overcome and he is interested in flaws not just for the sake of the vulnerability itself, but what process could stop that vulnerability becoming a bigger problem, at the business level. He works as part of a team and is keen to influence those who need security, but don't necessarily know it. He is a technologist that is also focused on people and process, which is why he is embraced not just by the cyber security community but also by the business community.

A final word: Keep a learning mindset

Carroll spoke earlier about the importance of learning the fundamentals of the industry. This relates to something that Lance Spitzner spoke to me about:

> I would tell my younger self to be open-minded and learn as much as you can. Try everything and learn from everyone in this field: the more knowledge you gain, regardless of the field, the stronger you will be.

Learning as much as you can about cyber security, whilst not putting pressure on yourself to know *everything*, will stand you in good stead for your whole career. Kenneth Geers spoke to me about this, too:

> Always try to learn new things, especially outside of your comfort zone. As an analyst, I have often neglected to develop my technical skills. It's OK to focus on something, but there are many other areas in which we can improve our understanding – which also helps you to succeed in your own, narrower field of study.

For Freakyclown, this broad approach to learning applies not just to learning about cyber security, but to learning in general:

> If I could give advice to my younger self, it would be to read more; one of my advantages has been consuming books. It is a fantastic way to gather distilled information. I was an avid reader as a kid and into my teens, but as I reached adulthood work got in the way and the rate at which I read dropped. Nowadays, I try to cram in as many books as I can, sometimes four or five a week if I'm travelling a lot. I also recommend that people experiment with consuming educational materials; for example see if you can get used to watching videos on a faster playback speed. Two very influential books for me were *Hyperfocus* and *The Go-Giver*, which helped me structure my days more effectively and think about the focus of my work. I also wish I'd learnt more about stoicism when I was younger; it's a great approach for managing stress and something which I think a lot of people in security would benefit from.

John Carroll spoke earlier about looking after yourself physically and Freakyclown's point about looking after your stress levels, which can impact mental health, is easily as important. Stoicism is a philosophical approach that is very applicable to modern life, and to those of us working in cyber security, with its focus on mindfulness and resilience, and thriving despite stress and hardships. Learning that goes beyond cyber security may help you make discoveries that are not only applicable to security, but that also help you on a personal and emotional level.

Jonathan Armstrong also shared some advice at the personal and emotional level, speaking about the importance of self-confidence:

> The advice that I would give myself that first springs to mind would be around dress sense – that could fill a small book. Aside from that it's probably to have confidence. I was the first person from my family to go to university. I think my mum and dad had been conditioned into the type of jobs they could aim for, and given where I am from, I think my younger self suffered from that too. My daughters were big fans of pantomimes – a recurring panto song is 'Reach for the Stars' – a cheesy song, but a decent life lesson, too.

I love this message from Armstrong. We can often look at people in life and find it impossible to imagine how we could achieve what they have, with many of us in danger of placing limitations on ourselves. I used to be extremely guilty of this until I came to understand that life puts enough limitations in our way, but if we work hard, creating and seizing opportunities that come our way, then we also generally find that life brings many good chances our way, too. Taking these chances can have a positive, snowball effect on your career and, with hard work, you can find yourself with opportunities you would never have dared dream of. I daresay that everyone, throughout the course of their career, will encounter people who try to limit or undermine them to some degree or another. Don't be that person, either to yourself or to others. Nurture your self-belief, your skills and the people around you. Understand that cyber security is a broad, and deep, field: you are not expected to know everything and worrying that you *should* know everything will only waste valuable time that could be spent actually learning more! Instead of questioning whether you know enough, or are skilled enough, follow your curiosity, learn about what interests you and share that knowledge with the community. You will be amazed at what you achieve.

Notes

1 It is policy for the NCSC to only use first name and first initial of surname publicly.
2 A vCISO is a virtual chief information security officer. They are generally security practitioners who work for an organization on an ongoing basis, generally part time and sometimes remotely; they often provide these services to many different organizations at the same time.

Appendix
Answers

Exercise 0.1: Decoding the message (page 4)

The key is 13 right (or 13 left!) and the message should read:
This is an example of a Caesar cipher. Well done for decoding it!

Exercise 1.1: Assessing the risks (page 37)

A multinational bank

The information an international bank will handle includes personal and financial information of customers, money transfers, personal and financial information of personnel, and intellectual property. Of course, on top of this, banks hold physical money and assets.

Attackers that are most likely to target them include financially motivated cyber criminals, hacktivists, script kiddies, nation-state-level attackers and malicious insiders.

A political party

The information a political party will handle includes personal and financial information of members and donors, plans and strategies for the party, internal (potentially sensitive) communications of the party and internal financial data.

Attackers that are most likely target them include financially motivated cyber criminals, hacktivists, script kiddies, nation-state-level attackers and malicious insiders.

A *local estate agent*

The information a local estate agent will handle includes personal and financial information of customers and of personnel, and money transfers.

Attackers that are most likely target them include financially motivated cyber criminals, script kiddies and malicious insiders.

Exercise 5.1: Hot state triggers (page 100)

The red flags to look out for in this spear-phishing email are authority (the email purports to come from their boss), urgency/time pressure, confidentiality, a sense of closeness (the reference to internal fraud) and flattery (the target is the one person chosen by 'their boss' for this important and confidential task). Did you spot any of these in the exercise?

Index

Bold page numbers indicate illustrations, *italic* numbers indicate tables.